PERFECT
ORDER

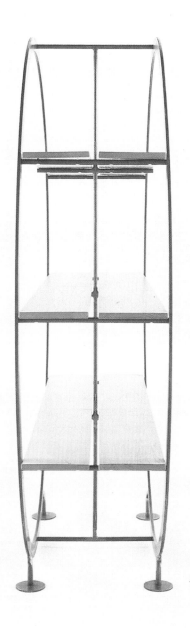

PERFECT ORDER

SIMPLE STORAGE SOLUTIONS

ELIZABETH HILLIARD

with photography by Ray Main and Laura Hodgson

SOMA

For my husband William, who has encouraged me to aspire to perfect order, in my life as well as in my home.

Text © 1998 Elizabeth Hilliard
Photography © 1998 Ray Main, Laura Hodgson, Christine Hanscomb

First published in 1998 by Kyle Cathie Limited. North American edition published in 1999 by Soma Books, by arrangement with Kyle Cathie Limited.

Soma Books is an imprint of Bay Books & Tapes, Inc.
555 De Haro St., No. 220
San Francisco, CA 94107.

For the Kyle Cathie edition:
Editor: Kate Oldfield
Editorial Assistant: Kirsten Abbott
Copy Editor: Ruth Baldwin
Design: David Fordham
Production: Lorraine Baird

For the Soma edition:
Publisher: James Connolly
Production: Suzanne Scott
North American Editor: Carolyn Miller

Library of Congress Cataloging-in-Publication Data on file with publisher

ISBN 1-57959-046-2

Printed in Singapore
10 9 8 7 6 5 4 3 2 1

Distributed by Publishers Group West

CONTENTS

INTRODUCTION

STORAGE CAN SET YOU FREE

IF YOU HAVE POSSESSIONS, you need storage to organize them and keep them in good condition. If you have well-planned, imaginative storage and plenty of it, you will find that you have more space and fewer worries. You will have created perfect order, which will set you free to enjoy your home and your life.

There is nothing so tedious as knowing that you have something, somewhere, in a cupboard or drawer, but you can't find it when you want it. You either have to do without, or you go and buy another, which simply adds to the problem. Another possession! Another thing to find a place for! Our lives are so full of things, things we love or need, or think we might need one day, that our homes fill up with them until we are in danger of feeling overwhelmed by the chaos and jumble of too much clutter.

Even if you are a tidy person, you know that possessions that are not well organized occupy more space than necessary, are not easily accessible, and take precious time to find. Life is too short.

There are some events that prompt us to rethink storage – a change of circumstances, for example. Perhaps you are getting married, and a home that has happily accommodated the life and belongings of one person is about to be filled with two. Or the arrival of your first child is imminent; or your family is expanding fast. Or you are moving from a larger home to a smaller one. Or someone you know takes holy orders, goes abroad, or dies, bequeathing you some or all of their belongings.

If you are planning the storage in a new home, or setting up home for the first time, you will be making a fresh start that many will envy. This book will show you a wealth of storage options, with clever ideas to help you create perfect order throughout. If, on the other hand, you have ever opened a cupboard or drawer and sighed at the sight before you, this book is for you – dedicated to transforming your home and your life.

Storing the family, storage for the home office and other work spaces, storage for urban living in limited space, storage in the ultimate kitchen . . . these are just some of the contemporary storage problems that this book sets out to solve.

Storage need not be just a tiresome necessity. Approached with enthusiasm, it can even be fun – a challenge to discover just how well organized you and your home can be. Whether you are striving towards minimalism or simply want to regain control of the family home, you will find guidance in this book.

More than anything, creating perfect order in your home involves commitment. As with giving up smoking or sticking to a New Year's resolution, there is no point in starting unless you have decided that this is something you can do, will do. Making the commitment is the most important part. Once you have done that, the rest can become a reality.

This is an ingenious and sculptural wine rack, a million miles from the traditional wooden affair. Constructed from brown leather, which you can polish to a glowing sheen, it hangs on the wall. It has pockets for six bottles, which balance one another perfectly if you insert them alternately from each direction.

The owner of this bedroom, opposite, has achieved perfect order, in one corner of his or her home at least. Hanging clothes are ranged on hangers according to length, shoes are paired on a low shelf, and wicker baskets acting as drawers provide storage for small items.

CHAPTER ONE

REGAIN CONTROL

A glorious jumble (opposite) of books, eggs and tea, jugs and teapot, grater, garlic, and even a pair of boxing gloves has been corralled in a shelf unit simply made from solid timber. On the right can just be seen a traditional pan stand.

Pigeonholes (left), or a similar system for separating small quantities of stationery, pens, and paperwork, such as invitations and bills, are invaluable for organizing the contents of your desk so that everything is readily accessible.

OF YOUR LIFE
PLANNING & ACTION

DON'T LET YOUR POSSESSIONS take you over. Regain control of your life. Sweep away the detritus of decades and get back to the real you. Storage can help you do this, once you have decided to tackle the problem. Storage can provide solutions: It can give you perfect order.

There are three steps to reorganizing your storage: facing up to the problem, planning the solutions, and, finally, putting them into action. This chapter considers the first two; the next chapter describes the campaign of action to help you regain control. It is worth recognizing, from the start, that this campaign is not without some cost in terms of time and money – after all, almost nothing worthwhile in life arrives without effort. At the first stage, it requires you to assess realistically, and face up to, the scale of the problem. You need to recognize that simply throwing up more cupboards is not the answer. Bringing order into your life requires a fundamental overhaul, a rethinking of the way you organize and store your belongings. Moreover, if reorganizing your storage is to have long-term effects, it has to be not just a one-time task. Successful storage is a way of life.

The second planning stage demands some serious exploration of the recesses of your home and some stimulating leaps of imagination. Don't allow yourself to get depressed. Keep the goal in mind. Think of the final, triumphant moment when each stage will be complete (whether it has been applied to a drawer, a cupboard, a room, or your entire home) and you will be able to replace your possessions with relief and survey your transformed home with an elating sense of achievement. Think perfect order.

Implementing successful storage into a home takes time. If moving into a new house, it is often best to wait and see which storage system will suit you and the house. The solution may lie in building generous cupboard space, or you may find that a few simple but effective ideas will suffice.

MAKING LISTS

IMAGINE YOU ARE A VISITOR to your own home, not necessarily from another planet but certainly from another sort of world – one where everything is neat, tidy, and organized and every possession has its proper place. Walk around your home and try to see things objectively. Take a pad and pen with you and make lists as you go – one for each room – noting the type and size of the problem and giving it a stress rating (the extent to which it irritates you), which will help you set your priorities.

Several different types of list are useful. The first is a list of trouble spots. Another is the list of wasted or "lost" space that could provide a site for new storage: between or beneath freestanding furniture, above doorways and windows, under stairs, in window seats, or on bare walls that could accommodate shelves, racks, or hooks. Yet another is a list of objects that catch your eye as you walk around because they are of doubtful use and little or no sentimental value – the "Dispose" list.

Make the problem list in two columns, writing in the second any possible solutions that occur to you as you walk around. Often, these will be simple and require little more than some time and attention. "Problem: piles of papers such as letters, old bills, newspaper clippings, theater programs, invitations, etc., on desk and/or floor. Possible solution: Throw away as much as possible, put cubbyholes or lockers on the wall above for current and pending papers, and file the rest, creating new files for new categories of paper as necessary. Get a bulletin board."

Other items are larger and may require the attention of a professional. "Problem: chaotic clothes closet. Possible solution: Commission professional carpenter to make shelves and racks to utilize space better; then sort clothes and shoes, and dispose of anything not worn in last two years." Most storage projects come somewhere in between, requiring a certain amount of sorting and rethinking, followed by investment in some flexible storage, such as boxes, plastic crates, a shoe rack or plastic-coated wire drawers of the type sold by many large home supply stores.

Yet another vital list for each room is headed "Frequency" and divided into "Rarely," "Sometimes," and "Often." How often do you use/play/refer to that pan/game/book? If it appears in the "Rarely" column, why is it in the most prominent position of easiest access? (Probably because you thought when you acquired it that it would be invaluable/ unstoppable/unputdownable. Experience proved otherwise.) Sometimes, the problem with storage of an item is simply that it is in a position for the wrong access category. Things you use most often should be in the best places, where you can reach them and put them away easily.

ARE YOU A TIDY PERSON?

ANOTHER PART OF FACING UP to the problem concerns not your belongings but you yourself (or yourselves, if you live in a family or with other people). Are you tidy by nature? If not, could you be tidier and better organized if your rooms were arranged differently or if there were more receptacles for your things, or more specific receptacles? The answer is probably partly yes, the other part being better self-discipline. There is no substitute for putting something down, or away, in its proper place rather than thoughtlessly plopping it down anywhere, to be put away "later."

If you are, like most people, medium tidy, you probably thrive surrounded by a certain amount of creative clutter. You like to have things at hand – your current book, the newspaper, your handbag or briefcase – and you like to have certain of your possessions out on show because they give you pleasure to look at. Rarer (and alarmingly impressive to everyone else) is the breed of person who likes almost every last thing hidden away in walls of cupboards concealed behind sleek, smoothly opening doors. This person gets top marks from the feng shui experts, who believe that clutter impedes the flow through your home of the life force, chi. If you are not a super-tidy person, there's no advantage in pretending to be. Be honest – decide who you are before you start planning your storage solutions.

The checklists at the end of this chapter are an invaluable reminder of the amazing quantity and variety of things a normal family home can contain, each of which requires a keeping place.

Lay all your lists out on a table, including the checklists (with the items that are not applicable deleted and any others added), and collate them to produce plans for:

1 your entire home
2 each room, including areas such as the garage and attic
3 individual problem spots such as overflowing cupboards

The first of these will be an overall plan of action, given that individual areas are covered in the following two plans. All three will set priorities and targets, which should be realistic and attainable so that you can regularly tick things off and gain a sense of achievement as your plan progresses towards completion. Without this, transforming your storage could start to feel like an overwhelming task that will never be finished.

If you are tidy enough to always have your clothes on view, an interesting coat-rack can take the place of a wardrobe. This one is a magnificent colonial-style example made from iron and wood, with a handsome cornice that makes it look important. A stainless steel or chrome-plated stand would look at home in a contemporary or minimalist interior.

Draw your room to scale and make cutouts of furniture and furnishings. Place them in various positions in the room until you are satisfied that you have the best possible arrangement (without the sweat of actually shifting your furniture around).

PLANNING A ROOM

WITH YOUR MIND brimful of ideas, start drawing plans. Measure the room, measure the furniture, and get the dimensions of any cupboards or other furniture you are considering buying to give you more storage space. Make a floor plan on graph paper, using cut-out shapes for the furniture and moving them around until you are satisfied with the arrangement. Make elevation plans too, showing how a wall or a whole room will look when the proposed storage system is in place.

To create a scale drawing, either a plan (of the floor) or an elevation (of a wall), choose a scale such as 1 yard to 1½ inches, or perhaps 1 foot to 1 inch, or another scale that allows your room to fit comfortably on one sheet. Draw the shape of the floor or wall accurately, using the measurements you have taken. Furniture and objects should be drawn on the same scale and cut out from another sheet of graph paper.

The purpose of these plans is to help you arrange the space efficiently and prevent problems before they occur. It may be, for example, that a bookcase or display shelves placed against a particular wall, though you thought them a good idea, actually make that part of the room too cramped for comfort. Positioned at the other end of the room, however, they have plenty of space, can be deeper than in the other position, and will leave space for comfortable chairs or a table.

THE PURPOSE OF STORAGE

DON'T FORGET THE PURPOSE of storage in all the excitement of preparing plans. The aim is to make your rooms cleaner and tidier, your life simpler and better. In one room this may mean hiding things away, in another it means bringing things out on display. Certain items need protection because they are fragile or valuable; you and members of your household need protecting from other things like sharp knives, cleaning materials, and medicines that are potentially harmful.

Planning also involves using a good deal of common sense. Instead of simply allocating all your possessions of one type to one room, think instead of ways of making them as accessible as possible and your life as simple as possible. Store toilet paper in several places around the house – near each bathroom, for example – and basic cleaning materials by each sink rather than in a central place, perhaps a utility room, from which they would have to be fetched each time you want them.

TAKING ACTION

THE THIRD STEP TOWARDS creating perfect order in your home is the campaign of action. Many people consider this to be the most exciting part, because it is where transforming your storage gets physical.

The campaign involves turning out cupboards and drawers and emptying corners you had almost forgotten about as well as the ones you use every day. It gives you the opportunity to dispose of piles of stuff that you have been dutifully hoarding – by selling it, giving it away, or throwing it away. It also allows you to let go of possessions that you have kept out of loyalty because they were given to you or (often even more burdensome) you inherited them.

Your plan of action will probably involve reorganizing not just the contents of cupboards and drawers but entire rooms. It is also quite likely to involve some expense. You may want to buy elements of a storage system such as wire racks for the kitchen or cardboard magazine boxes for a workroom. You may want to buy, build, or have built whole new storage facilities that better fulfill your needs – that are more efficient, more attractive, or space-saving.

Decide what your budget is for buying furniture and the services of professionals. Make a shopping list. Establish what you can do yourself in the way of assembling, installing, and possibly building things, and what you can't do yourself. At this point you may want to make a time-based schedule along the lines of "things we can afford and have time to achieve by Christmas," ". . . by Easter," ". . . by next summer," and so on.

If you are going to need the services of a carpenter, find and commission him or her well ahead, discussing costs and timing. A written estimate or contract, including drawings and material specification, is essential unless you are employing someone you know well and trust. Even under these circumstances, such a document is a good idea, from the carpenter's point of view as well as yours, in order to avoid misunderstanding and dispute in the future.

Workers such as carpenters, especially the good ones, are notoriously booked ahead and usually frustratingly unspecific about dates when they can actually start and finish work, because they don't know exactly when their previous jobs will end. If the job involves plumbing as well as carpentry, as may be the case in building storage in a kitchen or bathroom, ask the carpenter if he or she knows and works with any plumber in particular. Even better, hire a licensed contractor, who will give you a bid for the total cost of jobs involving more than one worker, and who will hire and manage these workers and the job as a whole.

These drawings show how you can fill an otherwise "dead" space with a cupboard (above) for storing small items, or shelves (below) for displaying objects. This window has a sill lower than the bottom of the window frame, creating an empty well. With a bit of imagination, this is transformed into useful storage.

Storage at home is a little like politics. There are national politics and there are local politics. Sometimes the route to solving the national problems is by addressing the local ones, but often the issue requires action at a national level, with sweeping changes whose effects are felt at every level. The most interesting problems also usually require attack from several different angles at once, whether in politics or the home. This is undoubtedly the case with storage.

CHANGING A ROOM

TAKE THE CASE OF A LIVING ROOM that never seems to be tidy, even after it has been "tidied." This may be because there is simply too much stuff in it, some of it suited to the "Dispose" list, and not enough storage space. But there may be a more fundamental problem. Is the room being used for many purposes at once – as a television room, a playroom for children, a study for the person whose desk is in the corner, a book room for the entire family?

If this is so, a radical solution is not only to reorganize the room itself, incorporating more storage space and hiding television and music equipment, but also to separate off some of the room's functions. Put a video machine for children's videos with a television in another room; place plastic stacking boxes for toys in a corner of the kitchen to make a play area; have shallow bookshelves in upstairs passages to accommodate large numbers of small and paperback books; convert a spare bedroom into an office-cum-spare bedroom (the two uses are often mutually exclusive). Think of these changes as "space management."

This array of built-in drawers covers a large expanse of wall, and is impressive not only in external appearance. There is space here to store a vast quantity of possessions, but the owner must have an excellent memory to remember what each drawer contains, as they are not labeled.

REORGANIZING SPACE

SPACE MANAGEMENT is fun because it provides almost instant solutions. Take a long, narrow room, where the furniture and cupboards are arranged around the outside. By dividing it up, visually and practically, into areas for different activities, you can create useful storage space.

Create a seating group at one end, with the sofa placed across the room and a generous two-tier occasional table in the center, in which you can store board games or magazines, for example. At the other end, create a work or children's area, with a low cupboard of similar proportions to the sofa backing onto it. Pulling seating away from the

walls often liberates wall space for storage. The principle is the same in other rooms such as bedrooms, where rethinking the arrangement of furniture may have a similar liberating effect.

SYSTEMS

ANOTHER KEY TOOL in organizing storage is the system. A system is a means of separating a great mass of things into many smaller types or categories and keeping them that way so that they are protected, accessible, and you can see at a glance what you've got (stock control). Systems work in every room in the house.

A utility room, for example, is an ideal candidate for systemization. You could create effective storage not only by putting up shelves on a currently blank wall, but also by building on this success with a system of clearly labeled boxes on the shelves for bulbs, candles, fuses, metal polishes, wood polishes, shoe-cleaning materials, rags, dusters, bottles of house-cleaning materials, backup stocks of laundry and dishwashing soaps, rubber gloves and hand cream, sewing and mending materials, and that refuge of the uncategorizable, "miscellaneous."

Creating systems is a necessary preamble to reorganizing your home. When you empty a cupboard and sort the contents, you don't want to put the things back on top of each other as they were before. Instead, you need to have a system ready to receive them. Beware of being inflexibly systematic, however.

You may assume that the obvious way of organizing possessions of one type – linens, for example – is to keep them together in one cupboard, but this may not be the most efficient method of storing them. Storing things in the various places where they are used may well be the better option. In the case of linens, you might prefer to keep tea towels, napkins, tablecloths, and the like in a drawer in the kitchen for easy access, and bed linen for particular bedrooms actually in those rooms. This would make space in the linen closet for other things, such as soaps that will scent the remaining linens.

CONTAINERS

THERE IS A WONDERFUL ARRAY of containers available to help you create storage systems, and it is worth exploring all these possibilities, in shops and catalogs, before deciding on one. The most widely available is the plastic box. This comes in many shapes, sizes, and designs to fit in every imaginable cupboard and on every conceivable shelf. Some have handles, others lids.

These drawers (above) are useful for storing very small items in a systematic way, to which end many of them are labeled. Above and below the drawers is a display of pretty antique chinaware.

Bookshelves, built from floor to ceiling, offer copious storage space, with the books themselves organized by subject and author.

Plastic crates, one of the most useful inventions of the late twentieth century, are here clearly labeled not with words, but with images, which even a child can use to identify the contents and locate the required items.

A charming antique pharmacist's cabinet has many small drawers, each with a tiny enameled plate to indicate the (former) contents. Today, it houses a collection of tiny items, and some also sit on top.

Some stacking boxes (supposedly for recycling or toys, but their possible uses are endless) have one end sloping or opening out so that you can access them without having to disturb the stack. Other boxes are smarter, less utilitarian in appearance, and covered with fabric or decorative paper, which may make them suitable for more visible locations. A huge range of boxes is discussed in the chapter devoted to them (see page 48).

All sorts of other containers are useful too, and a few of them come free, which is a bonus. These are usually forms of product packaging such as large plastic candy jars which, if you are lucky, your neighborhood or corner shop will give you free when they are empty – a form of recycling. Cookie tins, shoe boxes, and cans can all be useful. Wash and dry the latter and make sure that there are no sharp edges, then paint them to create colorful containers for crayons, pencils, scissors, or wooden spoons.

Baskets (rarely free) are another popular and versatile container for creating systems. These are most often wicker, sisal, plastic, wire, or plastic-coated wire and can be on show or inside cupboards or drawers. Many wicker baskets will fray and fall to bits eventually if they are not treated with care, and there is a risk that they will stain the contents and the surface on which they stand if they get wet. All baskets are useful as containers for fresh vegetables, as they allow the air to circulate through the holes.

LABELING

LABELS ARE VITAL for creating systems and they can add a bit of decorative fun. You can buy them colored or embellished or make or decorate them yourself. They can also be interesting shapes. The most important element is the writing, which should be legible.

Include detailed information on your label – you will find it useful later on. Give the contents a general heading and a date, and list the items individually. Then when you want one particular item, you will be able to find it without the frustration and wasted time of searching through several boxes.

SORTING CUPBOARD CONTENTS

BUYING FURNITURE and the services of professionals are grand gestures. On another, and just-as-important level, the time has come for some serious sorting. First, prepare the relevant system of containers; then you can get down to turning out the contents of closets, cupboards, drawers, and piles of stuff half-forgotten in corners.

Before starting, take some or all of the following steps:

- Buy a supply of plastic sacks, large stick-on and tie-on labels, and a marker pen.
- Find out when the local auction house has its sales of antiques and general household goods over the coming months, what the terms are, and how far in advance you can deliver things.
- Have boxes or old suitcases ready to receive clothes or other items that you really believe are worth keeping long term, and an anti-moth agent.
- Find out where the nearest municipal dump is for large items.

- Find out if there is a local garage or yard sale soon (or have a sale in your own backyard).
- Establish where the local charity shops are, what goods they accept, and when you can deliver them.
- Find the nearest secondhand clothes shop or designer-wear agency and establish what items they will accept, what their terms are, and when you can deliver.
- Set aside a decent amount of time so that you are relaxed when making decisions.

Boxes under a bed provide quantities of easily accessible storage. Several boxes, rather than one large one, are good for children because their toys can be sorted into different crates and each is not too heavy for the child to pull out.

PARTING WITH PRESENTS

OFTEN, THE REASON people put off clearing out cupboards and closets is that they dread having to make decisions about possessions that have a history. They feel disloyal getting rid of wedding presents, guilty about throwing something away that might yet be useful, and they can't quite face chucking out all those diaries and letters that meant so much during the angst-ridden teenage years.

PUTTING STORAGE IDEAS INTO ACTION

Be brave. Be realistic. Put yourself first (the person you are now, not the one you were ten, twenty, or more years ago). You haven't displayed the albeit charming china dog your great-aunt gave you in the last eight years, so you aren't likely to start now. If there is still use in something, let someone else use it who actually wants it. Are you ever, ever, going to reread your schoolgirl diaries ('We had sausages for lunch today . . . Mr. Simpson smiled at me in math class . . .'), one glance at which now makes you cringe?

Playing games such as "Do I need it on the boat?" can help you be decisive. Imagine you are moving into the home of your dreams, a magnificent houseboat moored on the river in the heart of London/Paris/anywhere. Storage space is strictly limited, and you might sink if you take too much with you (allow yourself some poetic license). This type of pretense can clarify which of your belongings really matter to you, and which don't.

If it will help, enlist a friend, someone who will be supportive and dynamic. Invite him or her over and open a bottle of wine. Why not? This is an important occasion. You are freeing yourself from decades of clutter and launching a new, lighter-weight version of yourself on the world. There are even professionals who will help you clear and sort your things, but if a friend will do it, you will probably have more fun.

THE ALL-OUT METHOD

A SUCCESSFUL TECHNIQUE for sorting a cupboard or drawer is the all-out method. This means, literally, getting the whole lot out onto the floor or table immediately, rather than taking things out one at a time. The sight of the empty cupboard will inspire you (and you can clean it). Be extremely careful what you put back.

Have various labeled bags ready for the charity shop/sales/garbage and so on as appropriate. When you have finished, remove the bags from the room, to the car or trash, so that the bags themselves do not form a new pile.

Seven options for dispersing the possessions that currently fill your storage space:

- throw away

- recycle – shoes, clothes, books, etc.

- give away to charity or a friend

- give away in the future as a present

- replace – only if it fits into storage plan

- sell, through an agency or secondhand shop (clothes), auction or dealers (antique items), rummage sale (junk)

- reorganize – put it somewhere else in the house where it will be safe, useful, or attractive, or with others like it

* Decide a budget for buying furniture and the services of professionals.

* Decide what you can do yourself.

* Make a time-based schedule for completing work.

* If you need a carpenter, book him or her well ahead after agreeing on the specifications and price for the job.

* Think about space: Is there a room in your house with too many activities crammed together? Can some be separated off into other rooms?

* Space management means rearranging the furniture in a room to create more space for storage among other things.

* No more clothes dumped on the floor: Have a bamboo (or other) ladder leaning against the wall and drape your clothes over the rungs.

* Plan systems for organizing many small items into groups.

* Consider all the types of containers for storage, including boxes, baskets, bags.

* Be prepared with plastic bags before you begin to empty cupboards and drawers.

* Be brave about disposing of things you have been keeping for years but realize you do not want any more.

* Sort your papers: Dispose of those that are out of date and archive as many more as possible to make space for storing current work and documents.

CHECKLISTS

Here are some useful lists of things to remember when planning your home-wide storage. Why not photocopy them so that you can delete/add items as necessary?

Clothes
Everyday clothes for each person
Evening and party clothes
Dressing-up clothes for children
Working clothes for painting,
    gardening, etc.
Vintage clothes packed away
Best children's clothes for future
    generations
Overalls to protect children during
    messy activities

Shoes
Everyday shoes for each person
Outdoor shoes
Special shoes – evening
Slippers

Outdoor Wear
Coats and raincoats
Boots
Socks, hats, scarves, and gloves
Umbrellas

Sports
Clothes and footwear
Equipment
Towels

Clothes Care
Clothes brush or roller
Dry-cleaning fluid
Extra coat hangers
Laundry soap
Fabric conditioner
Hand soap
Delicate-fabrics soap
Plastic bucket or bowl
Iron and ironing board
Starch, etc.
Shoe-cleaning equipment

Bedding and Bath Linen
Sheets and comforter covers
Valances
Pillowcases
Blankets
Bed covers
Comforters, pillows, and eiderdowns
Bath towels and hand towels

Cookware
Sets of pans
Other pans
Sieves and colanders
Measuring cups and scales
Mixing bowls
Cutting boards
Casserole dishes
Implements and knives
Baking sheets, baking dishes,
    roasting pans
Electric and other appliances

Other Kitchenware
Trays
Placemats and coasters
Oven mitts
Aprons
Tea towels and hand towel in current use
Napkins in current use and napkin rings
Cutlery
China
Serving bowls and platters
Carving board
Candles and candlesticks
Dish soap and other sink-side
    cleaning materials and tools
Rubber gloves
Fire extinguisher

Drinking Vessels
Mugs, cups, and saucers
Wineglasses
Tumblers and other glasses
Decanters and jugs
Tea- and coffeepots

Food
Dry staples: flour, sugar, etc.
Bottles of oil, vinegar, etc., for cooking
Dry goods: pasta, dried beans, etc.
Teas and coffees
Canned food
Perishable food in refrigerator
    and freezer
Vegetables
Bread

Food Preservation

Plastic wrap for refrigerator and freezer
Boxes and bags for freezer
Labels and ties
Aluminum foil
Parchment paper
Plastic bags

Seasonal Food Equipment

Picnic hamper, boxes, plates, etc.
Plastic jugs and glasses for outdoors
Grill and grill tools

Drink

Alcohol
Nonalcoholic drinks
Bar tools

Table and Kitchen Linen

Dishcloths
Tea towels
Napkins
Tablecloths
Aprons

Cleaning Materials

Disinfectant, bleach, and detergent
Floor cleaner
Dish soap
Dishwasher powder
Scouring pads
Toilet cleaner
Window cleaner
Mop and bucket
Buckets and bowls

Scrub brushes
Vacuum cleaner and spare bags
Carpet cleaner and soap
Brushes
Cleaning cloths and dusters
Polish
Air fresheners

Recycling

Glass
Glass bottles and jars awaiting reuse
Steel cans
Aluminum cans
Plastic containers and others for
    children to make models from
Paper
Books
Clothes and shoes

Books and Magazines

Telephone directories
Address book
Cookbooks and recipes
Reference books: atlas, dictionary, etc.
Maps
Guide books
Reading books
Magazines
Journal

Games

Board games
Playing cards
Chess, checkers, etc.
Outdoor games

Toys

Children's loose toys
Dollhouse, castle, or other structure
Children's pens, crayons, paints
Paper, coloring books, etc.
Construction models, glue, paint, etc.
Kites
Balls

Hobbies

Clothes
Footwear
Equipment

Household Administration

Files for bills for electricity,
    telephone, etc.
Files for bank statements, used
    checkbooks, etc.
Warranties
Instruction manuals
Daily planner
Address book
Record of presents given and received
Christmas-card list
Record of children's education: school
    reports, etc.
Keys
Glue, tape, and string
Current shopping list and pen
Shopping bags
Paper and plastic bags and shopping
    bags for reuse
Paper and pen for messages, etc.
Sewing kit

Home Office

Computer
Computer manual(s)
Software disks
Modem, fax, etc.
Paper, cards, envelopes
Used envelopes for reuse
Scrap paper
Labels, stickers
Address book
Mail-order catalogs and records
Filing tray
Filing system for correspondence
    received
Pens and pencils
Pencil sharpeners and erasers
Stapler, hole punch, scissors
Rulers
Desk lamp

Electrical and Light

Light bulbs
Candles
Matches
Batteries
Adapters
Extension cords
Fuses
Flashlights

Entertainment

Television
VCR and videos
CDs, cassettes, and records
Camera and film
Video camera
Photograph albums
Photographs not in albums

Medical and Emergency

Telephone numbers
First-aid kit
First-aid book
Fire extinguisher(s)

Bathroom Kit

Soaps
Sponges and/or flannels
Loofah/back brush
Bath/shower gel/bubbles
Personal lotions and potions
Toilet paper
Bath mats
Scales
Toiletry bags

House Maintenance

Tool kit
Paint, brushes, and brush cleaner
Stepladder

Bags

Suitcases
Backpacks
Handbags
Briefcases
Trunks
Daypacks

Garage

Spare tire
Jack and other car tools
Bicycle and helmet, etc.
Bicycle tire repair kit

Pets

Dog towel
Pet beds
Pet food and bowls
Litter box
Brushes
Toys
Leashes

UP STORAGE I:

The Shakers have become famous and revered for the storage system that they devised for their own needs. Only simple pieces of large furniture sit on the floor. Everything else is lifted up onto the walls.

The peg rail is vital to Shaker storage, but the idea can be used in any modern home to provide up storage for toys, bags, or as in Shaker homes, mirrors, candlesticks, and small furniture.

OFF THE FLOOR

THE PRINCIPLE OF UP STORAGE is refreshingly simple: Get your possessions up off the floor and other surfaces, and you free the space they occupied. Now, you also have the opportunity to sort out and organize the things themselves – on shelves, in racks, on hooks, on top of furniture, on ceiling-hung contraptions. Once you have done this, your possessions look much more appealing and are more accessible than they were when they lay in a heap. Where before there was chaos, you have now created perfect order.

An extreme, but extremely effective, form of up storage is the bed platform. In a child's room this could be a bunk bed with no bottom bunk, leaving a play area underneath with space for toy boxes and perhaps a table and chair. In an architect-designed studio, a "bedroom" can be built into the ceiling space, assuming it is sufficiently high, freeing the floor beneath for a kitchen, bathroom, or workspace (see more about this in Chapter Thirteen, page 150).

Most up storage is concerned with possessions, however. Our first reaction when we have something in our hand is to put it DOWN – in a cupboard, in a chest of drawers, on a table. Consequently, in many rooms in the home, wall and ceiling space is underutilized as a location for storage. The exceptions to this are generally in a kitchen, where wall-mounted cupboards are common, similarly in the bathroom. Shallow wall cupboards, often fronted with mirrors and useful for storing bottles and tubes, toiletries and medicines, are an acceptable part of bathroom furnishing.

This undulating wall sculpture (right) is actually a row of pegs. Lit from below, their forms create a ripple on the wall.

The storage of towels (far right) in a bathroom is a perennial problem. Here, it is solved by having a narrow radiator recessed into the wall with towels arranged across it.

This custom-built tie rack (below) will be the envy of any man who aspires to perfect order. A collection of ties is impressive, so why hide it away? The owner can see at a glance his choice for the day.

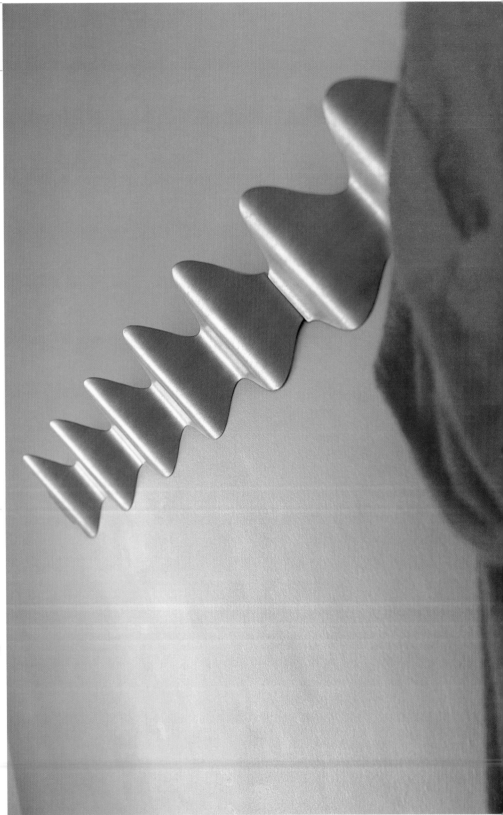

The simple plate rack, for drying dishes after you have rinsed them, is no longer an old-fashioned gadget. It has been reborn in many forms and made from, or finished in, various materials that are entirely at home in the contemporary interior, including wood and chrome plating.

A folding rack is invaluable in any kitchen, but especially a small one, because it can be put away flat and stored neatly when the counter is needed for other activities, such as chopping ingredients for cooking. Store the rack in a place where it will be close at hand.

IN THE KITCHEN AND UTILITY ROOM

THE CHAPTER FOLLOWING THIS is devoted to shelves – a huge subject in itself. But shelves are not the only solution, of course. Some objects can be just as well stored on hooks or racks – and they may often look more interesting as a result. A pan stand, for example, shows off a set or collection of a similar type of cookware – enameled cast iron or stainless steel – and frees cupboard space for storing all your less visually appealing utensils.

Pan stands are now widely available in various materials, including painted cast iron and chromed metal wire. Because it is a relatively tall and narrow contraption, a pan stand can transform a small corner of a kitchen or one side of a large open hearth into useful storage space. A pan rack could also be built horizontally across the top of a kitchen window to make use of that often-overlooked space.

Plate racks combine two functions at the same time: drying and storage. They are generally made of wood, with a vertical slot for each plate formed by upright wooden bars. Large country houses in the nineteenth century generally had a whole room devoted to storing various patterns of china for many different uses and occasions, one entire wall of which might house plates and platters in this way.

Today a plate rack is simply practical and attractive, but if you prefer you can hide it in a cupboard with no bottom (so that the water drips down) over the draining board or sink. You can also have a plate rack with bars wider apart, to accommodate cups and saucers or other wider pieces of china.

Another type of drying rack is the creel, for drying laundry indoors. No modern invention has surpassed the usefulness of this age-old contraption, a ceiling-hung rack with wooden bars. It is suspended from two points where ropes from the rack pass through pulleys on the ceiling. The ropes, which meet at the wall where they are secured by being wound around a cleat, enable you to lower and raise the rack as required. Just as the plate rack may substitute for or supplement a dishwasher, the creel may be used in place of or in addition to a clothes dryer.

A similar ceiling rack, made of wood or metal but not adjustable, has been a feature of country kitchens for hundreds of years. Pots, pans, and other cookware were hung from it; hams and bacon could be stored suspended from it. It was even used to store bread in cottages in Yorkshire and other parts of rural England, where unleavened bread was draped over the bars to dry. As the week passed, the bread, known as havercake, became dry and brittle, and members of the household would help themselves by breaking pieces off.

Such racks are once again available and popular for country and country-style kitchens in houses with a high enough ceiling to accommodate them. Some incorporate an enclosed area where you can keep bottles of oil, vinegar, and other attractively packaged cooking ingredients.

Other racks attach to the kitchen wall. These can be made from wood (a panel of trellis or a duckboard will provide an instant, inexpensive rack), metal, plastic (popular in the 1960s and still to be found cheaply in junk shops) or hardboard punched with rows of holes (peg board). You hang pans and tools from these by means of double-ended hooks (like butchers' hooks, but without the sharp points) or, in the case of peg board, using specially designed bent metal pegs. A single rail can do the job too, in a more confined space. Towel rails in bathrooms provide a form of up storage. and so can radiators of the "ladder-up-the-wall" type of design.

A spice rack on the kitchen wall is an invaluable form of custom-designed up storage, deep enough from back to front for only one or two jars containing herbs and spices. Once again, precious counter and cupboard space is set free for other things (and the jars are prevented from disappearing to the back of the cupboard until long after they are stale). Special wall-mounted rack dispensers for paper towels, plastic wrap, and aluminum foil are similarly effective, as is a knife block or a magnetic rail attached to the wall or the side of a full-height kitchen unit or cupboard.

The wine rack has become the subject of contemporary designers' attention. No longer is the choice between a grid made of wood or plastic, sometimes with metal structural supports at the back. Modern racks are almost pieces of sculpture and are made from leather, stainless steel, acrylic — a whole range of materials that will take the weight of bottles full of wine. Some stand on a work surface or cupboard, some on the floor; some hang from the wall.

A creel, or hanging rack that you can lower and raise with ropes and a pulley, is a wonderfully simple and old-fashioned way to dry your laundry. No family home should be without one. It requires only a strong ceiling (attach it to beams or joists) that is of sufficient height to operate it successfully.

The CD rack is a vital accessory for anyone with a sound system. It can be a traditional side-by-side arrangement, as above, or take up less worktop space by stacking the discs vertically, as below.

Racks are not confined to kitchens. The cupboard or room that stores your cleaning equipment would benefit from one of the many special wall- or door-mounted wire racks designed to get ironing board, iron, or vacuum cleaner off the floor.

RACKS IN OTHER ROOMS

In an office or at your desk, a rack for storing a small quantity of frequently used stationery makes it easily accessible while keeping it in order. Store the bulk of your stationery elsewhere in a cupboard or drawer. Another useful up storage device for any room, including the office, is the wall-mounted swivel arm designed to take the weight of a computer monitor, television, or video recorder.

As with the wine rack, so with the rack for storing music recordings on cassette or CD. It has been transformed from a dull plastic box (cheap and useful when hidden in a cupboard) into a sculptural entity made from any suitable material that catches the designer's fancy.

HOOKS

HOOKS ARE INVALUABLE up storage devices. The range now available far surpasses that of just a few years ago, when the choice seemed to be between brass double hooks for the back of the door, gnarled and blackened rustic hooks thought suitable for country homes, and little sticky-back plastic hooks for . . . what? Tea towels? Every bedroom and bathroom door should have a hook or hooks on the back for hanging up a dressing gown or bathrobe. A utility-room door should have a hook large enough for storing spare wire coat hangers awaiting shirts and other garments fresh from washing or ironing.

Whatever your decorating style, there are now handsome, practical hooks and racks to suit it, from black iron racks of the type originally found in French farmhouses, to 1950s-inspired zigzag hooks with brightly colored plastic knobs, to retro chrome racks from old train compartments. Some of these are modern, some are genuine antiques. Junk shops and salvage yards offer fruitful hunting grounds for the latter.

The basic cup hook is essential for efficient storage, not only in kitchens but also in workrooms, even playrooms and bedrooms. A piece of curved metal, one end of which has a thread and a point so that it can be screwed directly into the side or bottom of a

Racks can be bought or built in to your own exact requirements. This one is on the wall and used not only for drying but also for storing china. Small mugs dangle from the bottom, suspended on butchers' hooks in an ingenious, individualized storage system.

shelf or beam, the cup hook is available in many sizes and finishes. If you don't like the finish, you can of course paint it.

Besides doing what its name implies – storing cups or mugs by hanging them from the underneath of a shelf – the humble cup hook can store any kitchen gadget suspended from a sufficiently (but not too) low ceiling, as well as baskets, bags, tools (in a workshop or tool shed), and anything else practicable. In an old house with exposed beams, a nail hammered in can do the same job.

A row of hooks is useful in almost every room in the home. The most beautiful example of this is perhaps the Shaker peg rail. In a Shaker home, the peg rail ran around much of the room, allowing not only items like clothing and household tools to be hung, but also furniture like chairs, in order to clear the floor for sweeping.

A row of similar hooks equipped with coat hangers can take the place of a wardrobe in a spare bedroom that is only occasionally used; a row placed low on the wall inside the back door encourages children to hang up their own coats; in the kitchen a row accommodates not only aprons and a dustpan and brush, but also bags of empty bottles and plastic containers for recycling. Best of all, in a playroom (or bedroom) a row of large hooks on the wall will store play furniture, bags of modeling clay and equipment, doll carriages, and strollers – anything, in fact, that will hang on a hook.

Up storage is not only useful but vital in children's rooms, and Chapter Ten, "Storing the Family" (see page 112), deals with these in detail. For adults, a look through home supply and decorating shops, magazines, and mail-order catalogs will reveal rich pickings in gadgets for up storage. Of course, gadgets are not always necessary: A stack of old leather suitcases, decorative hat boxes, or attractive blankets and quilts folded in a pile, stored on top of a cupboard or wardrobe, is just as effective.

IDEA BOX

RACKS AND HOOKS

* Get things off the floor to free the space they occupy.

* Something lying on the floor is more likely to get dirty, be damaged, or forgotten completely.

* Your possessions look more appealing on a rack or hooks than they do in a heap.

* Wall and ceiling space in the home is often underused as storage space.

* Types of racks for the kitchen and utility room include the pan stand, plate rack, pan hanger, spice rack, creel, and racks for iron and ironing board.

* Hooks and rows of hooks are available in countless styles, including French farmhouse, Shaker, 1950s, and modern stainless steel.

* Find genuine retro racks like those from old train compartments in architectural salvage yards and junk shops.

* Do not overlook the many possibilities offered by the basic cup hook and nail-in-a-beam.

* Use hooks to help children learn to look after their clothes.

* Hooks can be used to lift children's toys off the floor in a playroom or bedroom.

* Racks for adults include wine racks and wall-mounted swivel arms for television, video, and/or computer.

* The choice of racks for storing videos and music recordings is enormous – some are like pieces of sculpture in themselves.

UP STORAGE 2:

A view through shelves (opposite) to the kitchen and living room of a cleverly designed small London flat. The cupboards are off the floor, which increases the sense of space.

The bathroom of another flat by the same architects, Littman Goddard Hogarth. The shelf is glass but so is the panel behind, which backs on to the living room where it introduces "borrowed" light.

SHELVES

OGETHER WITH CUPBOARDS and drawers, shelves are the mainstay of a storage system designed to deliver perfect order to your home. One of their charms is that they can be relatively cheap and easy to install. On the other hand, you can choose to commission a unique contemporary shelf unit from a cabinetmaker. Shelves also look as good covering an entire wall as they do confined, for example, to a small, pretty antique bedside bookcase.

The top half of walls in a room is often underused for storage purposes. Shelves provide the ideal solution. Why stop at the top of the door, after all, when you can continue a wall of shelving right across the top? If there are shelves on both sides of the door, this arrangement will have the added advantage of unifying the wall visually. The top shelves should obviously be home to the least-used books, to which access is not a priority, or the boldest objects, because smaller ones will not be well seen. In the kitchen, space above the refrigerator is often wasted (at best there is a precarious pile of things that have no other home balanced on top) and could be used if shelves were installed.

The same principle applies to windows. It is possible to make use of the wall above a window, simply by building a shelf across it, and perhaps all around the room, in the manner of a plate shelf (though not necessarily for displaying plates). The position of the shelf or shelves depends on the architectural proportions of the room, but in general, unless the ceiling is very high, an over-window shelf looks best with a simple window treatment – shutters or blinds – or bare.

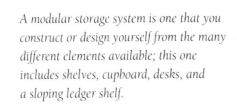

A modular storage system is one that you construct or design yourself from the many different elements available; this one includes shelves, cupboard, desks, and a sloping ledger shelf.

Several units in this system (left) have glass doors to protect the treasures stored on display within. These lift and slide back, disappearing along the ceiling of the unit, when access is required.

This bathroom employs industrial shelving. This is another modular system, here constructed with no low shelves, to allow space for a laundry basket and towels to be stored beneath. Unusually, this bathroom is equipped with a television on one of the shelves.

Every detail of this kitchen has been meticulously planned and designed. The shelves across the window make use of the space, while displaying a few beautiful pieces of cookware. Each shelf is unusually thick and has a front edge cut away for greater elegance.

"Our maxim is that you can never have enough storage," says the co-owner of this stylish and contemporary apartment on the top floor of what was once a dog-biscuit factory. The mezzanine was specially built, and at the planning stage, it was considered vital to provide the flat with ample cupboards for storing everyday items as well as gadgets and accessories.

The mezzanine has sufficient storage space to house, in the large custom-made cupboards built in underneath, everything from miscellaneous cleaning equipment to a dazzling cocktail cabinet that has been lined with leopard skin–printed fabric. The apartment is a lesson in making the most of all available space when planning a well-ordered home.

This was once part of a Thames-side sugar warehouse in London (above). Bookshelves have been built cleverly from the waist up, leaving the wall below plain white to increase the sense of space.

The drawing room of this family home (right) is lined with bookshelves, which embrace the double doors. There are even books stored on top of the cornice.

A simple but magnificent bookcase unit is used to divide living quarters from sleeping quarters in this contemporary loft apartment (right), or perhaps the floating wall was planned first and the idea for shelves came afterwards.

Start your shelves about 1 foot above the floor, and make use of the intervening space by having drawers in which you can store a clutter of small things (left).

TYPES OF MATERIAL

ASHELF OFTEN SUPPLIES the simplest and most versatile solution to storage prob-lems. Common sense needs to be used to make sure that your shelves are right for the load, and are properly supported; the advice of your supplier should also be helpful in making such calculations. In general, the thicker the material from which the shelf is made, and the deeper the shelf from back to front, the greater the load it can bear. Hardback books are heavy, glassware is light. Shelving materials do vary in rigidity, however (see below).

There are three separate elements to a shelving arrangement: the shelf itself, the type of support for the shelf, and the fasteners to the wall. Shelves can be made of a great variety of materials, to complement different interiors, including:

Storing and displaying items on glass shelves (left) enables you to see all sides of them, including the bottom, which may well be of interest if the object is fine bone china.

Wooden shelves (above) can be veneered, with a thin layer of wood glued to board, or, as here, solid timber that ages beautifully but is considerably more expensive in the short term.

WOOD

- Hardwood. This is the most expensive option but also, in some circumstances, the most practical. It will weather and age beautifully. Hardwoods such as oak are more rigid than other timber types and will bear fairly heavy weights (over a suitable span) without bending.

- Softwood, such as pine, is a more popular choice because softwood is cheaper, indistinguishable from hardwood when painted, and sufficiently strong for normal domestic use for short to medium spans.

Other types of wood-based materials can also be used to make shelves:

- Plywood is cheaper than softwood, strong, available in waterproof form, and popular with contemporary designers.

- MDF (medium-density fiberboard) is made from tiny sawdust particles compressed with glue. It cuts like butter, so is easy to work, but the dust should not be inhaled. MDF gives a superbly smooth surface for painting or varnishing and is available in various

thicknesses. A waterproof type is obtainable that is essential for bathrooms, kitchens, and other potentially damp places; the normal type swells up when wet. MDF is not especially strong, taking only light to medium loads over a short span (depending on the depth and thickness of the shelf), but it can be strengthened with an angle iron across the back edge and beading or edging across the front.

- Melamine-covered composite. This is also inexpensive and practical, but not aesthetically pleasing. Useful in utility rooms and workshops.

Melamine (below) can do a good job in the right context.

METAL

- Painted metal. Inexpensive painted metal shelving units for self-assembly at home are fantastically useful and available at almost all home supply stores and hardware stores. They come in various basic colors and black, but you could paint them yourself to match a special color scheme.

- Galvanized metal. Small metal shelves are useful in workshops and kitchens with a high-tech decorative theme. Beware of sharp corners and rusting (this should happen only if the surface is scratched or damaged).

- Other metal shelving is available, constructed from such materials as

Galvanized metal shelves (above) look smart and are waterproof. This one has an upturned edge that prevents objects from falling off accidentally.

ultra-modern chromed wire and retro wrought iron (of the type seen in French bakers' shops).

OTHER MATERIALS

- Glass. Use toughened glass to help avoid accidents. Only suitable for light loads, glass shelves for displaying objects can look splendid when well lit, either artificially from above or below, or with natural light if they are installed across a window. Colored glass looks stunning displayed in this way, as the glass shelf allows light to show off the glowing colors to maximum effect.

- Acrylic. This is a clear material that looks and feels like plastic. It has many of the qualities of glass without the weight, but is more liable to scratch.

- Slate. A slate shelf was a traditional pre-icebox method of keeping food cool and fresh in the home, and it still works today in a pantry or cupboard. You could also use slate to make a handsome mantel shelf (many nineteenth-century mantelpieces have slate shelves that were originally painted, often with faux marble) or even shelves in a small alcove. Slate is heavy and needs substantial support.

This white shelf appears to float on the wall, but metal rods actually give it sufficient support to carry medium-weight items.

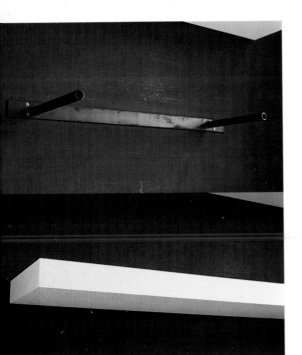

Methods of Support

Shelves are either supported at the ends or jut out from the wall, supported from the back, or they are supported at the back and sides, as with batten construction in an alcove. They are either adjustable or nonadjustable. The nonadjustable systems are better for carrying heavy weights, though the track-and-bracket adjustable system is almost as strong.

Adjustable Shelving

- A slotted metal track is countersunk into side supports, or screwed onto it. Small, flat clips, available in a variety of types and colors of metal, slot into this, supporting the ends of each shelf. The track can be painted (be careful not to clog the holes, which are already narrow), and the look is sophisticated without being invisible. This and the method below are suitable for fairly short spans carrying medium weight.

- A peg system, where the shelf ends are held up by pegs made of wood or metal, for each of which there is a hole in the side support. You can drill the holes at regular intervals down the supports, or only in the places where you know you need them now. More holes can easily be drilled in future when you want to alter the shelves' positions.

- A wall track, into which slot brackets that support the shelf from the back, taking considerable weight. Brackets can be bought in various sizes for varying depths of shelves. Lower shelves could be deeper, higher ones shallower for ease of access. This is the cheapest, most utilitarian, and potentially, the least aesthetically pleasing system. If the shelves were painted wood, however (as opposed to melamine-covered), shelving of this type would be perfectly acceptable (and thoroughly practical) in a playroom, child's bedroom, or office. The track and brackets are usually silver-colored, but they can be sanded and painted (separately from each other and the shelves, so that the paint does not glue them together), though the paint might chip and scratch easily.

Nonadjustable Shelving

- In the strongest of these shelves, the end of the shelf is slotted into the side supports. Once the front of the supports has been finished with a beading or edging, the joints are invisible, so the appearance of this type of shelving is smart and sophisticated. Its construction should be left to a professional or an amateur with considerable experience of cabinet-making — other systems, such as some described below, are more easily executed by the layman.

The classic wall-mounted track system has been interpreted many times, here giving a sophisticated contemporary look.

- Hidden fasteners. Shelves with these have, if possible, an even smarter appearance than the type described above, because they appear to be without any visible means of support. There are two types of hidden fasteners: those that protrude into the ends of the shelf, and those that protrude into the back of the shelf. The first type is simpler, weaker, and consists of curved wire brackets that are fixed to the wall and fit into a slot previously made in the end of the shelf. The second type is heavy duty, both in relative terms of what it can support and also in terms of the construction work required to fix it in place. Steel rods are inserted into holes drilled into the (solid) wall at intervals along the length of the shelf-to-be. The front two thirds of each rod sticks out from the wall, and on to these is slotted a shelf with ready-prepared holes. This type of construction is best left to the professional or experienced amateur.

- Wooden battens. These are narrow pieces of wood screwed to the wall and side supports, giving the shelf near all-round support. Sometimes the side pieces are angled at the front ends and stop short of the front of the shelf in order to be visibly discreet.

- Fixed brackets. These vary from the mass-produced to the craftsman-designed. Every hardware and home supply store stocks certain types, such as the utilitarian stamped metal bracket and the curved wooden bracket. More exclusive designs, varying from the classic to the inventive, are made from a wide range of materials. In between these two alternatives is the simple timber bracket constructed from three pieces of batten: one fastened to the wall; one projecting from the top of the first at a right angle to it, to support the shelf; and the third cutting the corner between the other two, spreading the load downwards. This traditional triangular bracket is simple to make.

- Other types. If you have a small, lightweight shelving unit to hang on the wall, use concealed hanging plates. The plate can be painted the same color as the wall so that it disappears. This type of support is suitable only for light loads. Yet another type of shelf has its support built in. Such shelves are useful in the kitchen for holding small jars.

IDEA BOX

PRACTICAL MATTERS

* Metals shelves include bare, painted, and galvanized finishes.

* Transparent shelving includes glass and acrylics.

* Consult your supplier about the load your chosen material will bear, and adjust your ideas accordingly.

* A shelf for keeping food cool can be made from marble or slate.

* Adjustable shelving systems include countersunk slots, a peg system, and brackets in a wall track.

* Nonadjustable shelves are those supported by battens, fixed brackets, hidden fasteners and shelves built into the structure of a piece of furniture.

* When choosing fasteners for shelves, take the material from which the wall is built into consideration.

* Check the route of electrical and water supplies before starting work.

* Bookshelves and CD racks need not be straight-up-and-down wooden affairs: Some are curved on the wall, some spiral up from the floor, some are made from shiny metal, and others from wire or plastic.

* Small suction shelves (and soap holders) stick to the tiles in a bathroom.

* A hammock made from plastic or nylon netting, suspended from the bathroom ceiling or high up on the walls, stores stacks of children's bathtime toys.

CHAPTER FOUR

DOWN STORAGE

An interesting low coffee table (left) by the designer Ray Davis. Entirely made of MDF, apart from the hinges, it has six compartments, each with its own lid that lifts to reveal the contents. The colors are stains, sealed afterwards.

Even the grate in a fireplace can provide storage space, here for a collection of handsome shells. In summer, or in a room where the fireplace is redundant but attractive, fill your fireplace with found objects large enough not to fall through.

U P STORAGE IS CONCERNED with getting things up off the floor and other surfaces, and using walls and even ceilings more efficiently as storage space. Down storage, as its name implies, is concerned with creating order by stowing things away, in and under furniture and fittings. It is a way of using your floor more efficiently, by reusing space already occupied by something that has another use. Down storage makes the most out of furniture so that it gives extra storage space along with its traditional use. Some down storage can be added on to a room, but other types usually have to be built in – an example of this is a window seat whose cushioned top removes or whose lid or front is hinged to reveal generous storage space beneath/behind.

The possessions that you place in down storage will be different from the ones in up storage, where things are out in the open, often on show. Up storage is best for things that stand or hang upright, like clothes, books, objects, and vases. Down storage generally keeps things out of sight and is useful for things that lie flat, like linens and blankets, as well as for objects stored in a jumble, like children's toys or balls and bats for outdoor games. For this reason, there is a danger that the jumble will become a muddle and the things at the bottom will be lost or forgotten. Guard against this by resisting the temptation to fill the space too full. Half-full or a little over gives you enough scope for moving things around for access or to see what there is. Storing items in an orderly fashion with, for example, pillowcases in a separate pile from sheets, will make finding them easier, too.

Shallow drawers (above) are built into the risers of this set of steps. A small hole in each in lieu of a handle allows you to pull them open.

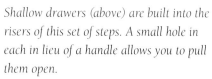

The space underneath the wooden slats of a bed (above right) is used for storage of items that are rarely needed, such as Christmas decorations.

The floor of this bedroom was raised to accommodate a bath beneath the bed as well as copious under-floor storage in spaces like the one that exists beneath this pull-up hatch.

Tucked behind the kitchen door, this cupboard with elegantly curved doors gives a neat ending to a row of kitchen units topped with polished marble. China and miscellaneous books are stored inside.

The space under the bed offers an obvious opportunity for down storage such as these deep drawers.

This still life is formed by coats hanging on pegs, tall umbrellas standing to attention in a bright plastic container, and a basket containing outdoor shoes.

OUTDOOR BOOTS AND SHOES

PEOPLE WHO LIVE IN THE COUNTRY in temperate climates generate boots and outdoor shoes that are wet and occasionally covered in mud. Where to store these is a perennial problem. The solution is to find a warm, dry spot near the door where they are out of the way and are not going to be kicked over. Under the coat-rack or hooks is a suitable place, provided the hooks are high enough so that the garments do not brush against the boots, picking up damp and mud.

Store the boots and shoes on a rack several inches above the floor so that air can circulate around them to help them dry out. The rack should either be on a hard floor, onto which drips of water and lumps of mud can drop without causing damage, or there should be a tray on the floor to catch the drips. The tray can be removed for cleaning, or the floor beneath the rack can be swept with a brush or vacuum cleaner.

In hotter climates, place a receptacle that is attractive, can easily be cleaned, and can be lifted to clean the floor underneath by the outer door ready to receive outdoor footwear. This could take the form of a simple rack, something like a wooden duckboard, for example, or a box or basket.

UNDER THE BED

ONE OF THE MOST OBVIOUS, and most popular, examples of down storage that can sometimes be added on as an afterthought is under-bed storage. A bed is usually either a freestanding frame, a platform, or built in. Each of these types offers potential for down storage. A freestanding frame has plenty of space underneath – the challenge is to make the things stored there accessible if need be, and to protect them from the dust that gathers under unfitted furniture.

Some of the items that are suited to under-bed storage, such as seasonal clothes or bedding like winter blankets, do not need to be particularly accessible. You need to reach them only once a year when you want to retrieve them. These could be placed in a large, box-shaped zip bag – one of the many types of storage bags to be found in shops and mail-order catalogs – and pushed far under the bed. Some such bags are made of clear plastic or have a clear plastic window so that you can see at a glance what is in them.

Under the bed is the perfect place to put your gift store, where you keep the presents you have bought your friends and family until Christmas or the day of someone's birthday

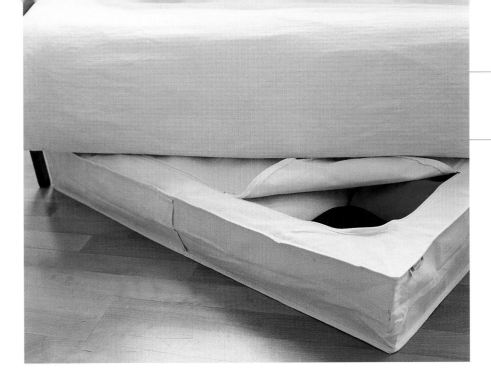

There is now a huge choice of bags designed to help you store every imaginable item in every corner of the house. This is a large under-bed bag with a zip top (a lid of some sort is vital for keeping out the dust), providing a useful place in which to store winter bedding and clothes in summer.

arrives. For items like these, which need to be accessible, there is the wooden or plastic under-bed box on wheels or casters. These are widely available, in a great range of sizes and styles, but you could use any box you consider suitable. The type of flooring in the bedroom will be influential – for example, wicker baskets will not slide so well on a carpet or rug as they will on a wooden or other smooth floor.

As a means of moving the box, casters or swiveling wheels are more versatile because the box can be pulled out in any direction; ordinary wheels can go only backwards or forwards in one direction. Ideally, this box should have a lid, otherwise dust will fall onto the things in it; alternatively, the items themselves can be individually boxed or bagged (preferably with at least a see-through panel, or you could spend some time rummaging for the one thing you want). The advantage of the latter method is that you don't have to pull out the entire box and lift the lid when you want something from it.

You will want to hide your under-bed storage (unless the receptacles are visually attractive – wicker baskets, perhaps – and in keeping with the rest of the bed's and the room's decoration). For this purpose your bed needs a dust ruffle, or bed skirt, a sheet that lies under your mattress, attached to which is a flap of material hanging down around the bed and covering the bed base. This skirt can be full length, brushing the floor, or shorter. It can either be gathered into a loose frill or hang straight and flat, perhaps with pleats at the corners of the bed, to give a more tailored look.

If your bed is a platform, you may have chosen one with drawers built into the base – if not, you cannot alter it and will have to wait until buying a new one to make the most of under-bed storage. A futon platform can be mounted on strongly built storage units containing a variety of cupboards and drawers. Similarly, a built-in bed should have drawers or lockers with hinged doors opening down, fitted into the base, much as they are on a boat, to take advantage of every possible area of extra storage. Similar ideas can be creatively applied to living in small spaces on land, a subject that is dealt with at greater length in Chapter Twelve (page 140).

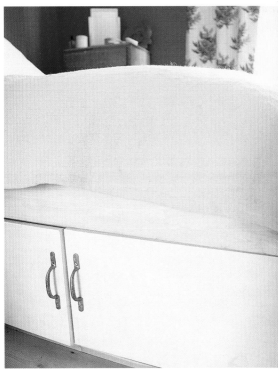

A custom-built bed platform with cupboards beneath gives plenty of storage space (above). A barge or boat can offer inspiration for using every possible nook and cranny as storage space.

A cupboard under the bathroom sink (above) can provide plenty of storage for toiletries, cleaning materials, and extra toilet paper, but it can make a small bathroom look cramped. Use the space underneath the end of the bath where possible.

Another example (right) of making constructive use of the space occupied by stairs. Each riser is the front of a drawer, which pulls out to provide much-needed storage space.

BATHS AND SINKS

BATHS AND SINKS offer opportunities for down storage. A simple curtain stretched around the front of a sink can hide bottles and jars or cleaning materials. Alternatively, have the sink boxed in to create a type of washstand with a cupboard beneath. Boxed-in baths can have a cupboard incorporated into the structure, usually at the head end of the bath because the slope at this end allows more space for children's toys or unsightly bottles. Paint the inside of the cupboard with a waterproof paint or varnish to prevent water from causing damage.

A cupboard built into one end of your bath boxing would normally be finished with one side against the end of the bath to prevent objects disappearing into the void under the tub. To maximize the storage space in the cupboard, build this side 6 to 12 inches farther towards the faucets, with a shape cut out of it to accommodate the curve of the bath.

Perhaps the most extraordinary example of down storage is the disappearing bathroom. In this case, a small city apartment was transformed and its living space increased by doing away with the bathroom completely. Instead, a toilet was installed under the staircase that went through the building, a sink was hidden in one cupboard in a wall of built-in storage, and the floor of the enlarged bedroom was raised enough to accommodate a bath sunk into the floor beneath the bed. The bed itself was on tracks, which allowed it to be pulled easily to one side when the bath was required. Other areas of the raised floor had pull-up hatches revealing more storage beneath – again, rather like that on a boat.

OTHER PLACES

BESIDES WINDOW SEATS AND BEDS, another useful site for down storage is the ottoman. This is one of those versatile pieces of furniture that fulfill more than one function. Not only is it a stool for sitting or putting your feet up on when relaxing; not only does it also, when you lift the hinged lid, provide storage; but in addition you can use it as a table on which to place a tea tray or a tray of drinks. Not all ottomans have storage inside – be discerning when choosing one.

Occasional tables often have a shelf beneath, which is another source of down storage, ideal for current magazines, books, and a box of writing paper and envelopes for writing letters while sitting on the sofa.

Blankets, eiderdowns, and other bed coverings needed in winter but not in summer are bulky objects for which to find a home. The blanket box is a traditional and ever-popular form of down storage that can double as a table or informal seating in a bedroom.

Large objects such as boxes (see also Chapter Six, page 58) can provide down storage that is interesting or beautiful to look at. A battered old leather trunk with labels from travels around the world speaks of romantic past journeys, as does an immaculately lacquered chest from the Far East. A hand-made beechwood box would be the equivalent in a simple, pared-down, contemporary interior. Containers that sit on the floor provide down storage for long, narrow items.

An unused fireplace can supply a form of down storage if shelves, drawers, or a cupboard are built into it. In a playful form of trompe l'oeil, the cupboard could have painted on its doors an illusory fire, lit and glowing merrily. Another unusual place for down storage is the staircase, where an architect could design drawers to be built into the risers, making use of the space beneath the treads (but care should be taken not to weaken the structure).

In a room with a sloping wall – in an attic flat or a room under the eaves – create cupboards by boxing off the lower half of the wall (or more). This will give you areas of flat wall against which to stand furniture, at the same time providing cupboard space for possessions. Even if the resulting cupboard is shallow (because the slope of the wall is not extreme), it will be useful for small items like drinking glasses, placed on shelves.

Magazine racks (above) come in as many different forms as there are designers devising them. Some fold away when not in use, some are made of wood (left), others from metal and wicker (right) or finished with chrome (center).

IDEA BOX

PLACES FOR DOWN STORAGE

* Boxes under the bed

* Built-in cupboards or drawers in a platform bed or under bed

* Window seats

* Inside an ottoman

* In a blanket box

* Built into an unused fireplace

* Under stair treads

* Under the bath and sinks

* Under the floor

BOXES, BAGS,

The humble cardboard box is now a glamour item in interior decorating. These filing boxes are covered in paper in a thrilling choice of brilliant colors, and would enliven any office or filing system.

Bright boxes are made in different sizes but also different shapes, to accommodate specific items like CDs, computer disks, cassettes, and your collection of family photographs.

AND MUCH MORE

THE BOX IS A WONDERFULLY SIMPLE THING: an object with flat or round sides, with a bottom, and often a top, designed to contain other objects. Endlessly useful for creating order out of chaos and frequently decorative and interesting in themselves, boxes come in every shape and size, from every country and period in history.

More than any other element of storage, boxes are made from a huge variety of materials: plastic, cardboard, paper-covered or fabric-covered, wood, wicker, leather, ceramic, acrylic, glass, stainless steel . . . The trick is to choose the right material to suit both your decorative scheme and the room's environment. Cardboard boxes stacked up in a utility room are far from ideal, for example, because this is likely to be a steamy room and cardboard is

not waterproof. Stainless steel is sleek and expensive and you probably therefore want it to be in a position where its shiny smartness is visible so that you see it regularly and gain pleasure from the sight: a perforated stainless steel laundry bin in the bedroom, perhaps, or decorative stainless steel storage canisters in the kitchen.

Boxes of every size have a purpose: tiny ones for storing (separately) the smallest things vital for modern living, like safety pins, cuff links, and postage stamps. Bigger boxes can hold gloves and scarves or jewelry in a bedroom, packs of cards and games in a sitting room, bottles and potions in a bathroom. Large box-like storage such as trunks and old suitcases are useful all around the house. A flat-topped trunk can double as a bedside table or a sofa table in a living room.

The photographs on these pages prove that one basket can be used to store a range of items.

Baskets are not only made of traditional wicker (above). Plastic, sisal and coir, wood (as in Shaker concertina baskets that fold flat), and metal baskets are all available. This one, which is used to contain nail-care accessories and polish, is plated with shiny chrome.

Metal (left) is a useful material for storing potentially dirty items like shoe polish, as in this basket. Mesh baskets are lightweight and easily transported around the house as necessary. Items stored thus in a drawer can be lifted out en masse.

Right: A wire basket like this was originally designed for storing cutlery, but will just as well hold a mass of small items necessary for an activity like dressmaking or sewing. Each compartment holds a few essentials such as spools of thread, a tape measure, scissors, and pins.

Hatboxes (above) stacked up like this in decreasing size are a charming way of storing anything, not just hats. These ones are not merely decorative, however. They are awaiting hats created by their owner, a professional milliner.

C A R D B O A R D B O X E S

CARDBOARD IS THE Cinderella of storage. A decade ago it was merely a form of packaging. Today, sophisticated storage boxes and systems are constructed from it by contemporary designers. You can build stacks of cardboard drawers that have smart ribbon or leather pulls, or arrange them in neat rows on shelves for a serious, archival look; your CDs, videos, and computer disks can be stored in glossy, brightly colored, paper-covered cardboard boxes; small items of furniture are even built of it.

Cardboard comes into its own in the office and attic. In the office, you can use cardboard boxes to store and organize almost everything that does not go into the filing cabinet. Use cut-away magazine boxes to store not only magazines but also items like mail-order catalogs, guide booklets, and other reference material. (In the kitchen, a magazine box is useful for storing cut-out recipes.) Newspaper clippings can be stored in the office in one of these or in a closed box – the latter is more secure and dustproof than an envelope folder. Stacked upright like books on a shelf, tall, narrow boxes storing paperwork are easily accessible, one of the primary functions of good storage.

Plain cardboard boxes can be painted to color-code the contents and to contribute to your decorative scheme – undercoat with an acrylic primer for brighter colors or to cover the manufacturer's mark, then paint with two coats of acrylic paint. (For more about using boxes in the office for archiving papers, see page 155.)

In the attic, cardboard boxes are perfect for storing items that you think you might need one day or your children might want (are you sure?). They are light when empty and they stack easily. Buy boxes from a moving company, as these are of good quality, designed to hold their shape while the goods are lugged from place to place. They also come in many sizes: smaller ones for books, for instance, and other heavier objects; larger ones for lightweight things; big ones for fluffy stuff like duvets and pillows. Alternatively, keep the boxes when you move – peel off or cut through the tape and they generally fold flat for easy storage until you need them.

Cardboard wine cases for storing lightweight objects are free when you buy wine, or perhaps may be cadged from a friend. You may want to reinforce the base of a wine case with more tape to make it stronger. For items to which you know you are going to want access, consider buying cardboard file boxes with lids. In this case, you don't need to untape and unfold the lid flaps each time you want to get in – much more convenient. These boxes are bought in flat packs; you assemble them at home.

You can store clothes in cardboard boxes in the attic, but old suitcases or an old chest of drawers may be better, as the garments can lie flat. This has the dual effect of lessening

These heavy-duty cardboard boxes (left) each have a webbing strap to secure them. Here, the repeating forms have a rhythm, while interest is added by the fact that each box has a different color or finish on the outside. This is also useful for quick identification of the contents.

crushing and making the clothes more easily accessible when you want to retrieve them. Even in the ideal environment, the life span of most cardboard boxes is obviously not as extensive as that of some other materials, especially if they are worn out by being handled often. Some really good-quality, stiff cardboard boxes will last for many years, decades or more, however.

Whatever the quality of cardboard, it is vital to label the boxes clearly. Boxes destined for the attic should be labeled on each side, so that you don't have to pull them out of the pile to find the writing. Cardboard boxes are ideal here – you simply write straight onto the box with a large marker pen. If you are really efficient, you could use different colored pens to code the contents of different boxes into types. Be as specific as possible when labeling. Don't just write "China"; write "Miscellaneous china vases and pitchers," or whatever, and a date when the box was stored. Apart from anything else, a date will help you be realistic when you clean out the space sometime in the future: "Is it really ten years since I put that away?..."

PLASTIC BOXES

THE PLASTIC BOX is one of the late twentieth century's great inventions, transforming household storage, especially in families. Plastic boxes have countless uses and are widely available. Every sort of shop seems to stock them, from the old-fashioned, small-town store selling various household wares and hardware to (predictably) giant home supply stores. Besides the many obvious uses to which you can put plastic boxes, like organizing children's toys and utility-room stores, they can facilitate recycling: Simply put the bottle, can, newspaper, or pair of old shoes in the correct box on a shelf in the utility room and forget about it until you take the boxes to the recycling center. Plastic boxes can also help you to make better use of deep shelves, and organize them more

Many types of plastic boxes come in colors, and some have lids. This is useful if you are putting the box under a bed or other piece of furniture, where the contents could get dusty, or high up. A lid also keeps the contents from spilling out when you lift the box down from a high place.

effectively, by gathering together items of one type so that they don't get lost in the miscellaneous clutter at the back. (For more about plastic boxes and crates, see Chapter Eleven, page 126.)

BOXES FOR SPECIAL JOBS

SOME BOXES ARE or were designed for a specific purpose, but do not have to be used for that purpose. Other boxes are needed for a specific purpose today. An example of the former is the hatbox: round, deep, and lidded, with a handle, intended for storing hats. Hatboxes are generally made of leather or paper-covered cardboard (you can re-cover them in your own choice of paper) and are often available in sets of different sizes. You can keep hats in them – or you can also keep anything you want. A stack of decorative hatboxes would make a handsome pillar of storage for small items in a bedroom: costume jewelry, gloves, socks, handkerchiefs, and so on. In a family room they could contain mail-order catalogs, newspaper clippings, letters waiting for reply, or old greeting cards for children to cut out and paste.

Boxes that we use for specific purposes include the sewing box, jewelry box, and tool kit. Any box of suitable, portable size and structure will do. A sewing box does not have to contain every item for sewing that you own. These can be stored in a drawer or cupboard in a utility or spare room; the sewing box is a transportable kit with the basic necessities in the way of needles, scissors, tape measure, pins, black and white thread and thimble, to which you can add items needed for the current job – colored thread or buttons, for example.

A jewelry box should contain only costume and other nonvaluable pieces. Valuable items should be hidden separately in various places (to confuse burglars) or in a safe. As well as traditional safes, which can be hidden behind a picture on the wall or behind a baseboard, there are "safe" boxes designed to pass unnoticed because they are disguised as other things, such as books or cans of food. You could make such a storage container yourself inexpensively.

The tool kit is a vital piece of modern household equipment. However magnificent the array of tools in your workshop or garage, it is practical to have a small kit in the house for instant access. A pair of pliers, a light hammer, a few screwdrivers, and a wrench will be invaluable for all the little jobs like re-fusing a plug or tapping a picture hook into position. A mass-produced plastic tool box is ideal.

Small trunks in regimented rows (below) look handsome. If you create a similar storage system, it is wise to label each trunk or box for easy identification of the contents. In this way, miscellaneous items can be ordered by group and stored away stylishly to give an uncluttered look.

SETS OF BOXES

SETS OF BOXES have a special visual appeal. Oriental lacquered boxes that fit inside each other like Russian dolls can be laid out in a row and used to store a series of small items for general household use, such as rubber bands, stamps, pins, markers, and so on. Or you could collect other ethnic boxes, antique snuff or powder boxes, antique visiting-card cases, modern boxes made from brightly colored plastic, or boxes of many origins but all in blue or red – any group with a clear visual link between them. Collections are special, too: old tins with the brand image printed on the outside – whether cookies, tobacco, or peppermints – are useful and can still be picked up in junk shops and at flea markets.

Use see-through boxes made from glass or some form of plastic to store contents that are visually appealing, such as costume jewelry or multicolored buttons. Clear shoe boxes are useful too, hidden behind wardrobe or closet doors. Likewise, clear storage bags for clothes are available, and useful for storing out-of-season garments.

BOXES AND BAGS FOR SHOES

THE ORDERLY STORAGE of the many pairs of shoes and boots that most of us accumulate is a constant problem. Some people like a rack in the bottom of their wardrobe, so that they can see all their shoes on display there. Others have rows of cubbyholes – one for each pair. Shoe boxes themselves can provide an inexpensive solution. Decorate the boxes by covering them with brightly colored or traditional brown paper, or paint them, sealing the color with varnish for a hard-wearing finish. Write a description of the shoe on the end, or stick a photograph or drawing showing the contents of each box.

In place of shoe boxes, you could use shoe bags. These have several advantages. They can be made of attractive material; they take up less room than a box; they wear well (they are washable); and when you travel you simply pick up the bag and put it in your case without having to remove the shoes and pack them separately. Labeling is, as ever, important for easy identification of the contents. Instead of gluing on a picture or drawing showing the contents, punch a hole in the corner and tie it on to the bag's drawstrings with a piece of colored ribbon or string. Alternatively, use a cardboard luggage label.

Shaker boxes (above), displaying the smooth, perfect ovals of their construction. Boxes such as these, made from solid wood, will age beautifully and give years of service.

Shoes could disappear without a trace in these boxes (below) stacked in a closet, if it were not for the designer, Spencer Fung's, bright idea of sticking a photograph on the front of each to indicate the contents.

BOXES, BAGS, AND MUCH MORE

This type of neat, handy rack with hooks below can be attached to the wall of any room. Here, it is home to an assortment of baskets above, with duffle coats and laundry bags below.

CLOTHES BAGS

ANOTHER TYPE OF BAG that is useful for storing elements of your wardrobe is the suit bag. This is generally made of impervious nylon fabric. The top is shaped like the shoulders of a coat hanger, and there is a zipper down the front. It comes in various lengths for different garments, and it is important that the bag is longer than the clothes so that they do not become crushed. Make sure also that there are small holes or an opening at the bottom through which air can circulate if the clothes are going to be in the bag for any length of time. Outfits that you rarely wear, such as formal wedding clothes or ball gowns, can be hung in such bags in the attic or a distant cupboard. Don't forget moth-proofing, and remember to air the clothes well before you wear them again.

Similar bags to these are available for other purposes, such as travel and the storage of numerous items together. For travel, zip-up clothes bags are available in more attractive fabric, colored or patterned, with strong zippers. For storing numerous items of clothing in an attic, there are hanging bags that are like portable wardrobes, with room for many garments suspended together from a rail or hook.

Ideally, a garment that is going to be stored for many years should not be kept in plastic. Brides have been known to store their wedding dresses hung up and wrapped in old duvet covers. An expensive but secure alternative for such a precious garment is to entrust it to a special dry cleaner who offers an heirloom storage service.

The laundry bag is an old-fashioned but popular form of storage, and not only for dirty laundry, though it continues to be exceptionally useful for this as it can be hung off the floor on a hook and takes up room only as it fills up with clothes. A laundry bag is also a useful item for travel, since you obviously can't take your laundry hamper with you in a suitcase. Schoolchildren can use small laundry bags for keeping everyday possessions like gym shoes, gym clothes, and a hairbrush together and in order in their locker or on their hanger at school or at home.

NET BAGS

NET BAGS HAVE MANY USES. The great qualities of a net bag include being lightweight and the fact that you can hang it up on a hook. Like the glass box, it also allows you to see what is in it. Made of cotton or nylon (waterproof), a capacious net bag with a drawstring is ideal in a family home for storing loose toys as well as any quantity of things that are bulky and go together, such as dressing-up clothes, modeling clay, and accompanying equipment, or empty toilet paper rolls and plastic packaging reserved for making models. In any home, net bags are useful for collecting and storing scrap aluminum foil, old greeting cards, and other small items generated in quantity by the family and destined for recycling or charity.

PAPER BAGS

LIKE CARDBOARD, the brown paper bag and shopping bag (and, indeed, brown paper in general) has experienced something of a style renaissance. A brown bag can be decorated and used as gift wrap; smart shops once again send out their goods in such bags; and they can be used for storing lightweight items at home. Simply hammer a horizontal or vertical row of nails into a beam or wall and hang small brown paper shopping bags from them. These can be used to store useful lightweight items such as other paper bags or used envelopes awaiting reuse, objects awaiting recycling, rubber bands, small rags, or luggage labels.

IDEA BOX

MATERIALS FROM WHICH BOXES AND BAGS ARE MADE

* Cardboard, paper.
* Plastic, wire mesh.
* Glass or clear plastic.
* Wood, leather, lacquer.
* Fabric.
* Nylon and cotton net.
* When choosing from the above, bear in mind that boxes made of translucent plastic or wire mesh seem to take up less space than ones that create blocks of color.

Traditional baskets are made in countless different shapes for different uses. This one is exactly the width of a wine bottle.

DISPLAY AS STORAGE

Left: An alcove designed specifically for displaying a tall, narrow object such as these lilies in a simple glass jar. The alcove is built into a partition and equipped with an adjustable spotlight.

The stairwell offers an expanse of wall on which to store and display a wonderful collection of hats that reflects the family's various interests and travels. A collection of objects looks best displayed together.

OUR POSSESSIONS SHOULD BE our pride and joy – if not, why have them? Of course, we all own things we have been given or have inherited and therefore feel unable to part with, for a while. There comes a time, however, perhaps after many years, when it is possible to free yourself from this heavy sense of loyalty. If you look at something and think, "I really don't like that," give it to someone who does. Do the original giver the credit of believing that he or she would not want a gift to be a burden. The test is: Would you put that object on display? If not, it may be time to usher it out.

Displaying one's prized belongings is a natural instinct. Only dedicated collectors of particular types of object are happy to hide them away for their sole personal delectation. To most of us, the pleasure of owning something is increased by seeing it frequently, and exhibiting it is a way of sharing that pleasure with our friends. Moreover, displaying these treasures is a way of storing them. Well-planned display keeps them safe and shows them off to advantage.

In a minimalist interior, with very little on display, those objects that are on show have added importance. In a brimful interior, the impact comes not so much from individual items, though these can be significant, as from the collective appearance of many things together. Most of our homes are somewhere in between. We have some single items that are interesting, and others that are best in groups or collections; some rooms are relatively cool and clutter-free, while in others the warmth and welcome that the room exudes comes from massed possessions.

DISPLAY
AS STORAGE

Another clever way of storing wine (above), provided by built-in triangular alcoves ranging up the wall. The effect is witty, the direction of the pyramids uplifting, and the rack makes wonderful use of what would otherwise be a tall, narrow gap.

In a sitting room (left), sleek storage units attached to the wall look as if they are floating, with no visible means of support. This allows the floor beneath to be seen all the way to its edge, increasing the sense of space. Having display space within the units and only displaying objects with clean, simple forms contributes to the ethereal effect.

A minimalist bedroom (right) has a neat, vertical row of display niches, here occupied by starfish. The orange object is a folding chair leaning against the wall.

Shelves have been built here specially to display a fine collection of antique china pudding molds and thereby to make constructive use of a passageway leading into the hall of this mellow country house. The shelves are painted a deep green, which shows off the white china.

A glorious mixture of colors and styles, with objects in one style on each shelf. Shelves across a window cut out some light but can provide extra storage; objects displayed there need to be well lit from the room or they will appear only in outline (except for colored glass).

Three different ways of arranging the same four framed photographs (a fifth has been introduced to the bottom group). If you have the space, try out arrangements of pictures by lying them on the floor before hanging the display.

WHAT TO DISPLAY AND HOW

WORKS OF ART AND CRAFTSMANSHIP are the most obvious category of object eligible for display in the home – not only pictures, but all manner of three-dimensional items. These are not the only things worth showing. Found objects that have intrinsic beauty, such as pebbles, shells, and gnarled wood collected on walks or holidays; everyday objects from other cultures; product packaging; antique or unique clothing or textiles . . . these and other kinds of non-art objects can be equally interesting.

Where and how you display your possessions depends partly on such factors as how much space you have, how many things you wish to display, and how fragile they are. One of the primary considerations of both storage and display is the preservation of your belongings from dirt and damage. Delicate items will need more protection than robust ones, but with proper precautions there is no reason why they should not be enjoyed by being on show. Be realistic: Don't put precious things at risk.

The same applies to possessions that have high financial value, if you are fortunate enough to own any. Your insurer may make blanket stipulations about how you store antique silver or a painting of worth. If these prevent you from displaying them to your satisfaction, consider lending these items to a museum or gallery, or discuss with your insurer or broker the possibility of displaying individual items at home. He or she may be able to suggest a compromise, such as an alarmed display case or picture hook, that satisfies you both. Simply screwing the picture frame to the wall in an inaccessible upstairs room may be enough.

As with storage in general, one of the keys to successful display is to group like with like. In the case of possessions on show, this rule is almost infallible. Even if you have only a few pictures, grouping them is preferable to dotting them around, however much larger a space they could potentially fill and even if this means having expanses of bare wall around them. This applies to objects as well as it does to pictures.

HANGING PICTURES

PICTURE HANGING IS A SUBJECT that makes many people nervous, and it is certainly worth doing well, but it need not be an alarming task. To start with, have nails and hooks that are suitable for the job: picture hooks with brass-headed pins, two hooks if the picture is large, hooks with two pins for heavy pictures. A stepladder and a yardstick

DISPLAY
AS STORAGE

6

A huge amount of care and imagination has gone into hanging the things on this wall; there is not only one collection of items but three – the hand mirrors, the antique prints and the collection of designer-shoe bags. The rounded shapes of the mirrors add relief from the squares of the prints' frames, and they have been placed in small groups for added impact.

or metal measuring tape is useful and so is a level, though the naked eye often does just as well. Don't rush the job – you don't want to make a mistake and have to rehang pictures. On the other hand, don't be afraid to do just that if they don't look right. It often helps to have someone to assist you, so that one of you can stand back while the other gives directions.

Make sure that the wire across the back of each picture is tight and does not show when the picture is hung. If necessary, tighten the wire or move the hooks that attach it to the picture farther down the frame (a quarter or third from the top is ideal). Check too that the wire and hooks are secure. Consider also the route of electrical conduits and possibly water pipes before beginning to hammer pins into the wall.

Each group of pictures should have an element that unites them: subject matter, artist, color range, style, or medium, for example. Don't be afraid to hang different media together (drawings, engravings, and photographs, for instance) if something else pulls them together (they are all black and white, say). A collection of pictures or objects will make an impression and need not be grand – photographs of your children or a line of old glass bottles acquired over the years, well displayed, will give you as much pleasure as a group of Watteau engravings would an art expert.

Plan where each group will hang in relation not only to where you sit in the room itself, but where you enter or see through from another room. Vistas can be created or made more interesting with a dramatic focus: a large or striking group, picture or object. The center or focus of each group should be at eye level or a little above. If you have high ceilings, do not be tempted to hang the picture or group halfway up the wall where you have to look up to see it. Lay your collection on the floor and experiment with arrangements. Hanging the group around an imaginary axis, which can be vertical, horizontal, or at an angle, is generally the most visually satisfying configuration. Start with the pictures nearest the axis, usually the largest, and work outwards. A friend is invaluable to hold up each picture in its proposed position for your examination before you hammer in the nail. Each time you add to the group, step back and examine your work.

An alternative to hanging pictures is to lay them under a sheet of glass on a table top or dressing table. This is an especially effective way of displaying a quantity of family photographs that give you a great deal of pleasure but that may not be so fascinating to other people.

DISPLAYING OBJECTS

O BJECTS OFFER MORE of a challenge for display than pictures. The simplest and most obvious way to show them is to lay them out on a surface, perhaps in a bowl or on a tray to combine them if they are small. This has several disadvantages and is practically impossible if you have small children. Depending on their position, the objects are not protected from dust and damage, and if you place them in safety on a high shelf it may not be easy to see them well. Consider some alternative solutions to their storage and display.

Attaching a shelf, shelves, or several single brackets each with a tiny individual shelf to the wall means that you can display objects in similar arrangements to pictures. Or it may be possible – and effective – to hang the objects directly on the walls, as with hats or plates, for example.

HANGING PLATES

T HERE ARE VARIOUS TYPES of plate hangers. One is a plastic-coated wire frame that has small, bent ends that grip the top and bottom of the plate; springs pull these tight (but not too tight) so that the plate can be hung by the frame from a regular picture hook. It's important that the wire is plastic-coated, so that the plate is not damaged by the bare metal. Another type of plate hanger is an adhesive disc that you attach to the back of the plate (but which should do it no harm and can be washed off). The disc comes in various different sizes for different weights of plate and is invisible from the front. The wire frame, though you can just see the ends, is discreet and thought by some to be more secure. Using either of these methods of hanging, you can make an attractive display,

An interesting collection of small curiosities is displayed very effectively by being brought together in a wooden box frame that is divided into separate compartments.

either of plates alone or of plates combined with pictures. China, or indeed pictures or books, can also be displayed standing on a shelf or piece of furniture, on a stand, or even on a small easel if particularly special.

BOX FRAMES

ANOTHER WAY OF DISPLAYING OBJECTS on the wall is to arrange and fix them in a box frame. This is simply a box with a glass front designed to be hung on the wall like a picture, to display collections. Box frames were popular in the nineteenth century for hanging collections of butterflies, shell pictures, and mementos of significant events. In the twentieth century, a few artists, most famously Joseph Cornell, have used boxes to make three-dimensional pictures.

Today, you could display delicate objects such as antique children's toys, small items of antique costume (away from daylight, which will rot fabric), or collections of objects with interesting shapes, like keys or spoons. You could also use a box frame to display something that needs to hang down to be seen clearly, or that would be shown off to advantage in this way: Simply hang the item(s) from the top of the box with clear plastic fishing line.

Box frames are now mass-produced and sold by at least one home store chain. Alternatively, you could make your own from a suitable box or from scratch. Paint the inside of the box, or line it with paper or fabric, in a contrasting color so that the object(s) stand out clearly before arranging them. They can be secured in position with tiny nails, on which they will rest when the box is lifted up to the vertical, or on narrow shelves, or with stamp hinges (if they are very light) or loose stitches in fine thread (if they are textiles).

THE BIJOUTERIE

A WONDERFUL METHOD of storing and displaying treasures is in a bijouterie, or vitrine. This is a table topped with a sheet of tough glass in a frame, a few inches beneath which is another surface, of glass or wood, on which your possessions sit. Either the glass lid lifts or a drawer pulls out beneath to give access to the treasures. It is, in effect, a sort of display case, a horizontal version of the box frame, with the added virtue of fulfilling the function of a useful piece of furniture.

Antique bijouteries can be found, but with difficulty. If you decide that a bijouterie is what you want, you may have to commission a cabinetmaker or even make one yourself.

A printer's tray has been transformed into the ideal display unit for a fascinating collection of antique product packaging. The lids tell us what was once inside; today they could be used to store pins, needles, and other tiny items.

Right: A textile designer stores her pieces of yarn, according to color, in bulbous glass jars like goldfish bowls stacked up on her desk. Their colors glow, lit both from behind and above, and help give inspiration for her work.

Above: Rows of jars containing a breath-taking assortment of buttons stand to attention across an entire wall, looking from a distance like so many jars of candies in an old-fashioned shop. The buttons do indeed look good enough to eat.

Your bijouterie will then have the advantage of being exactly in scale and in keeping with the style of your home. It could be made in coffee-table form, which will give you a generous display surface area and attract extra attention because you and your friends will regularly sit around it, or in a smaller, taller form, like a side table. You can, of course, change both the configuration and the entire contents as often as you want, and the bijouterie can be lockable to make it relatively secure and childproof.

MORE IDEAS FOR DISPLAY

CERTAIN ITEMS CAN BE STORED and displayed on or in objects that are themselves attractive and possibly even constitute a collection in their own right. If you wear hats, for example, you could keep these on old shop display heads or antique turned and polished wooden wig stands. Jewelry can be draped or clipped to a three-dimensional wire form, abstract or human, or kept in an engraved glass box. Cups and saucers can be displayed most effectively on antique plate stands, the more elaborate of which have pretty fretwork or carving.

DISPLAY IN THE KITCHEN

THE KITCHEN is one of the prime locations for display as storage (or storage as display). All that gleaming china, glass, and stainless steel – why hide it away? Be aware, however, that in the kitchen atmosphere objects will inevitably become steamy and greasy, however good your storage system.

For this reason, store and display glass well away from the stove. Of all possessions connected to cooking and eating, glassware advertises the presence of dust and even the finest film of grease picked up from the atmosphere. Shallow, open shelves, at around shoulder height, give you and the eye easy access to everyday items; less-used but nonetheless attractive objects can go on the higher shelves. Do not have everything on display, however, unless each single piece is in keeping with a strict visual theme: all cream, all blue-and-white, or all floral, for example. Hide the rest in a cupboard; otherwise the "display" can easily become a mess.

Gadgets and equipment can contribute to display in the kitchen, stored out in the open. Hang them along a beam, distribute them along a narrow shelf, or gather them together in a jar. As with china and glass, there should be a unifying visual element, probably the material from which they are made. Have all your wooden spoons and spatulas together in one container, your metal implements in another. Or hang your stainless-steel tools from hooks on a stainless steel bar, and range your gleaming set of knives along a magnetic strip rather than hiding it in a wooden block.

Food can look stunning. The shapes and colors of fresh fruit are luscious displayed on a three-tier stand made from wire or wicker – it will take up quite a space on a table or sideboard but is worth every square inch, especially if you want to tempt your children or guests. Dried beans or pasta shapes ranged along a shelf in transparent jars create a rhythm of interesting forms. Bottles of glowing oils and vinegars, some containing herbs or spices, are enough to inspire even a reluctant cook.

OTHER PLACES FOR DISPLAY

OTHER PLACES AROUND THE HOUSE have possibilities as areas for displaying your possessions. Waterproof items, especially anything that came from the seaside, can enliven a bathroom. A stairwell offers generous space for hanging a large collection of pictures, and added height for displaying something that is especially long or tall. Be careful, however, that it will not be knocked or damaged by passing shoulders. It is not unknown for the stairs themselves to be used for storage and display. A well-known comedian and her family keep their shoes here, one pair on each tread, each member having a step, in strict rotation, up three flights. A collection of rocks, large fossils, or other objects, substantial but not valuable, could be stored and displayed in the same unusual way, in a household where they are not likely to be thrown around.

IDEA BOX

SECURITY FOR THINGS ON DISPLAY

* Use proper picture hooks and brass-headed nails.

* Hang a large picture on two hooks.

* For a heavy picture, use larger hooks with holes for two pins.

* Use a wire frame or adhesive disc for hanging plates safely.

* Use picture wire strung between the eye hooks or D-hooks on the back of a picture. Do not be tempted to use string, as this will rot in time, causing the picture to come crashing to the floor.

* Consult your insurer about displaying valuable items.

* A box frame will keep delicate items safe.

* A bijouterie is a glass-topped table for displaying small objects safely.

* Keep textiles and watercolors away from sunlight, which will damage them.

* Show off your collection of postcards on a bulletin board – a magnetic metal one means you don't have to stick pins through them.

* Instead of putting your favorite clothes away in a closet, hang them on a tailor's dummy and enjoy them even when you are not wearing them.

* If you have young children, keep fragile or delicate items where they are least likely to come to any harm – which usually means displaying them at a sufficient height to be out of children's reach.

DISAPPEARING TRICKS

Left: Proof, if proof were needed, that the wall bed is up to date. This small city apartment has no spare bedroom; when visitors come, the bed is lowered and a sliding door provides privacy. Cupboards above store a duvet and pillows.

The same bed as opposite, folded back up to the wall. The frosted glass wall beyond it not only divides the bedroom from the kitchen but gives a good amount of borrowed light without any loss of privacy to guests when they stay.

Disappearing storage is the most fun to devise of any storage in the home. It involves playing tricks on the eye – now you see it, now you don't. The purpose of disappearing storage is twofold. Either it hides away things that are aesthetically displeasing or muddled in appearance, thus creating the illusion of perfect order, or it maximizes space by folding away or otherwise "disappearing." At its most elaborate and expensive, it can involve trompe l'oeil on a door or screen or a wall of specially built cupboards. Both options come into the range of the average pocket if you make them yourself or barter other skills that you possess for those of a professional muralist or carpenter. At its simplest, it involves having a hidden stock of folding chairs to bring out when you have friends visiting.

It is easier than you might think to commission an artist. Start your search in the small ads of home design and interiors magazines, or contact an artists' organization listed in the telephone directory or an artists' yearbook at your local reference library. See the work of several artists and get some idea of their relative fees before you commission. When you have made your choice, ask for a clear sketch or drawing before he or she starts work, and a contract of agreement including time scale and cost (this could simply be a typed letter signed by you both).

There are several spots in the home where disappearing storage is especially useful. The first of these concerns beds. Disappearing beds include sofa beds, futons, beds that fold up into the wall (sometimes known as "Murphy beds"), air beds, and trundle beds.

The bedroom in another flat designed
by the same architects as on the previous
pages, Littman Goddard Hogarth in
London. When all the doors are closed
(below), what you see is an unadulterated
wall of color, behind which are hidden
the bedroom and bathroom (above).
Folding doors take up less room than
full-sized doors that swing open.

The ultimate foldaway table, custom-made for this flat. The top folds up against the wall; the "legs" fold back, accordion fashion, into the space below. Even the dining chairs stack in order to save space. When the arrangement is closed, it looks just as handsome and interesting as when it is open.

The clutter of television, videos, sound system, and recordings is a perennial problem for the tidy minded, whichever room it is in. The answer, so often, is to hide it all inside a large cupboard, or on shelves with a blind that covers the front. These cupboards are vital for maintaining the severe simplicity of this interior.

A double bed with plenty of storage beneath, and space around it for objects and even a plant, has been created out of an unpromising alcove.

THE SOFA BED

IN A STUDIO APARTMENT or a spare bedroom that doubles as a home office or den, it pays to have a bed that can be used as a sofa during the day. An ordinary couch can serve this purpose, but the most obvious and popular solution is the sofa bed.

Sofa beds vary greatly in size and quality of bed construction and mattress. The most primitive is effectively a series of large shapes cut out of foam and encased in fabric – unfolded, it makes a low double bed suitable only for very occasional use. More sophisticated and comfortable than this is the type in which the sofa has a traditional wooden frame and the bed part unfolds out of the seat, the mattress resting on a mesh supported by a metal leg the width of the bed. You sleep on a pad of foam or, more substantial and supportive, a slim version of an inner-spring mattress.

In order to have a full-width double-bed mattress, the sofa itself is likely to be large – with arms it could easily stretch to over six feet in length and be correspondingly deep from back to front, though some designs are less bulky than this. Look carefully at the open and closed measurements of the sofa when you are hunting for the right sofa bed (take a tape measure with you). A two-seater sofa may give you only a single bed when folded out.

BEDROOM STORAGE

AN INGENIOUS METHOD of hiding bedroom storage is to use the bed board as a screen. Build a partition from floor to ceiling behind your bed and the same width as it. Behind this you can create a dressing area or install hanging rails and shelves for storing your wardrobe. If you share this room with another person, you could divide the space behind the screen in two and each have half, each approaching from your respective side of the bed.

THE FUTON

FUTONS ARE A DIFFERENT SORT of disappearing bed. The futon arrived in the Western world from Japan some decades ago and now has a growing and dedicated following of people who would sleep on nothing else. It consists of a wadded mattress made from several layers of fiber that generally include cotton, wool, and, often, polyester. The latter prevents the natural fibers from matting together over the years. You can lay the futon on the floor or on a basic wooden frame to allow air to circulate underneath. Both the frame and the mattress fold when the bed is not in use, with the space-saving advantage over a conventional sofa bed that there need be no additional structure (some styles of futon frame have arms). You can choose from a wide range of sizes and thicknesses of mattress, depending on preference and whether the futon is for daily or occasional use. Some users with back trouble like the firmness of a futon. Of course, you don't necessarily have to use a frame – the mattress can be rolled neatly on one side of the room during the day, as in Japan, or kept in a cupboard or chest. The air bed, complete with its own very fast pump, is a new alternative to the futon.

A sitting room, bedroom, wardrobe, and even a display area have been cleverly coaxed out of one tiny slip of a room. A ladder attached permanently to the wall gives access to the sleeping platform above, which is lined with bookshelves.

WALL BEDS

BEDS THAT FOLD UP against the wall have tended to have a rather un-chic, Depression-era image, and consequently they are often forgotten in the rush for other types of disappearing bed. This is a shame, as they offer another valuable possibility. You can buy one that is a counterbalanced, sprung bed frame, to which you strap your own mattress of the correct thickness, or one with its own mattress.

The bed can be placed in an alcove, hidden by a curtain, for example, or in a cupboard, or you can have a cupboard or faux front built to suit it. Paint the faux front the same color as the walls, screw a picture to it (on all sides, so that it doesn't swing out or fall off when you fold down the panel), and your bed will truly disappear. Such beds can also be bought already incorporated into one of many kinds of fitted furniture that include wardrobes and desks.

Wall beds are also available that fold against the wall not lengthwise, flipping up at the head end, but sideways, with a useful shelf across the top of the frame (which also serves to give it rigidity). There is even a pair of bunk beds available in this design. When the beds are closed away, you see two long, flat panels, one above the other, set against a tubular-metal frame. When they are open, the frame, which is substantial, supports the two single beds and also provides a ladder at each end for the person sleeping on top.

PULL-OUT FURNITURE

Secondary pull-out beds, or trundle beds, are those that fit under another bed. They can be built into the bottom of a stack of storage under a high-level bed, or bought built into a divan. In the best of this type, the second bed pulls out from a single bed and clicks up to the height of the first to make a pair.

Pull-out sections of other furniture make ideal hidden storage. The most widely available of these is the table with extra leaves that are stored under the main table top when not in use. Extending one leaf makes room for more people; extending both makes the table almost twice the size it is when completely closed. A kitchen, utility-room, or workroom counter can be built with a similar pull-out surface that is extended only when needed, as can an office desk (some ready-made desks have them too). A desk or table can also be built into the stack of storage under a high-level bed.

FOLDING TABLES

An entire table can be folded up or down against the wall of a kitchen or breakfast area, useful where space is especially tight. The factors to remember here are safety – you do not want the table falling down or folding onto the heads or fingers of a child (or indeed yourself) – and the fact that the table, even when folded, takes up that section of wall. The only other storage you could include in that space is an arrangement of shallow shelving or cupboards above.

Antique tea or card tables are designed to be placed against a wall, brought out for use only when needed. The top surface is unfolded to double the table area, and this then swivels, so that the legs support both halves of the top. Even opened out like this, however, they are relatively small, giving you dining space for a maximum of only four people.

Another type of clever antique table is the "Sutherland table," in effect a sort of folding coffee or tea table, wide and low. It is a form of gate-leg table, with a narrow center section of table surface, from each side of which hangs a wide, hinged leaf. When the

Well-planned shoe storage in the form of a unit that pulls out from behind cupboard doors. Each shelf then pulls out farther, allowing complete access to every pair of shoes. The entire arrangement is neatly fitted into a small alcove at the bottom of the stairs.

leaves are lifted, they are each supported by a leg that you swing out from under the center section (like swinging open a gate, hence the name). The gate-leg design is so effective that it is not only antique tables that employ it. The design is still used and popular today because such tables are easily stored, being quite narrow when closed.

Storage and space conservation are issues that concern many contemporary furniture designers, with the result that some intriguing pieces of furniture are available in modern design galleries and shops. Among the most celebrated of these is the Azumi table-cum-chest. Closed, this looks like a flat-topped A-shaped cabinet with two drawers above and below a shelf; open, it is a long, benchlike table with a drawer at each end. This sort of clever, witty design wins attention, awards, and customers.

Below: A prize-winning design by Japanese husband-and-wife team Azumi, this piece is called "Chest Equals Table." Its humor and versatility reflect the best qualities of folding furniture, which virtually stores itself – ideal for compact urban living and impromptu entertaining.

S T O O L S   A N D
F O L D I N G   C H A I R S

FOLDING CHAIRS are a heaven-sent accessory to modern living. No longer confined to the garden and the military campaign trail, folding chairs are made in a variety of materials including wood and canvas, metal, leather, resin, and tough plastics. The only qualification to using them is that you have somewhere to store them. This need not be a cupboard – some designs will hang on the wall on a Shaker-style peg or on a flat metal hook of the type intended for use in garages and industrial spaces. Stacking chairs save space too.

Stools are useful where space is at a premium, and not only folding ones. When not in use, a stool can be pushed away out of sight under a table. Flat-topped stools are especially versatile, as they can be used as occasional tables. Taller stools can also be used in this way, or to hold a lamp or electric fan, rather in the style of an antique torchère, a tall, narrow stand on which a candelabrum was placed to raise the light to a higher level.

S C R E E N S   A N D
O T H E R   C O V E R - U P S

DISAPPEARING STORAGE that hides the unattractive or simplifies the appearance of a room includes the use of doors, blinds, screens, and even curtains. The latter provide a cheap and easy form of cover-up. Curtains need not be fussy or grand. A simple calico curtain, layers of brilliantly colored saris or dyed linens, or even a delicate printed voile hung from a pole or rod can do the job in a contemporary interior.

Doors and blinds supply a flat finish. The advantage of the blind is that it doesn't require any space into which to swing open; this is also true of sliding doors, but they do not give you access to the entire storage space at once. All manner of possessions can be hidden in this way, the most obvious candidate probably being the home entertainment system, including television, video recorder, videos and music system with all its components, CDs, tapes, records, and so on. You may treasure every single part and still not want to look at the resulting clutter. There are many styles and designs of racks for music and videos, some of them attractive, almost sculptural, in themselves. If you are going to hide your system behind doors (or blinds or curtains), however, there is nothing to beat the basic plastic rack, which is compact, space-efficient, and wipes clean.

The folding screen has experienced a renaissance in the last decade. Previously, it was thought of as an old-fashioned item, covered either with découpage (popular in the

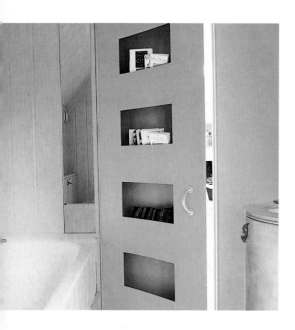

This bathroom door curves on the outside; inside, it is flat. The space between has been transformed into storage for bathroom clutter and even books to help the bather experience total relaxation. To keep everything from falling off when the door is swung open, access is confined to windows in the flat side.

A clever bathroom cupboard that takes up the whole of one side of the door. Closed, it is almost invisible. Open, it provides shallow but perfectly adequate storage for rows of bottles, tubes, and jars. The door of the cupboard should be closed when the door itself is swung open, to keep things from falling out.

nineteenth century) or with traditional fabric like toile de Jouy, which made it suitable only for homes filled with antiques. Interest in Japanese interior style has contributed to its new image as a versatile, portable piece of furniture. Now you can buy screens by the best new designers in contemporary materials, from bleached beech to stainless steel, while fabrics used are entirely in keeping with the contemporary ethic. An etched-glass screen will allow light through while masking the objects behind.

Screens have use in every room in the house. In a family room, you could employ one to hide the aforementioned clutter of high technology. A narrow screen with three or more panels can be arranged around a sink in a bedroom, so that the sink and toiletries do not detract from the style of the rest of the room. This could be a particular asset in a teenager's room, where she or he wants it to feel like a private sitting room into which to invite friends.

Ways of decorating a screen include painting it with a mural or design of your own, or painting it the same color as the walls before screwing framed pictures to it, of a type similar to others in the room, so that it blends in completely.

In a small, spare bedroom, a three-panel screen of slatted wood is the answer to providing your guests with wardrobe space. The slats can be used for draping smaller items like ties and T-shirts. Arrange the three panels in a U-shape, and larger clothes like dresses and suits can be hung from a pole placed across or near the top of the two outside panels. In a large bedroom, a screen with several panels can divide off an area into, say, a dressing room where a little more untidiness can be tolerated than in the rest of the room. The same would work in a studio apartment, where a screen could also shield a working area or a small kitchen.

IDEA BOX

FURNITURE THAT "DISAPPEARS"

* Sofa bed

* Futon

* Air bed

* Wall bed

* Trundle bed

* Table with leaves

* Gate-leg table

* Folding tables and chairs

* Stools

* Anything hidden behind screens, doors, blinds, curtains

CUPBOARDS

Opposite: A wall of storage cupboards providing a mass of cupboards and drawers of different sizes, constructed from MDF (medium density fiberboard). Here it shows its natural color, sealed for protection, but its smoothness makes painting it easy.

Left: A wall of drawers. Bringing your storage together into one part of the room, as here or opposite, leaves the rest of the room free of clutter and also means you can dispose of many small pieces of furniture that were formerly dotted around the room.

AND DRAWERS

ALONG WITH SHELVES AND HOOKS, cupboards and chests of drawers are the fundamental components of the storage system that will help you create and maintain perfect order in your home. They absorb and organize possessions in bulk, in every room of the house.

The great decision when considering cupboards and drawers for your home is whether to have them built in or be freestanding. As freestanding furniture they are, like boxes, often attractive pieces in themselves, with the advantage that you can move them around when you want to change the look of a room and take them with you when you move. Built-in units can be painted or finished to blend into their surroundings, but so can some cupboards.

CUPBOARDS AND DRAWERS

Below and right: When the doors in this wall of wood are closed, the bedroom's simplicity is complete. Open, they reveal the stairwell and, farther along, the bathroom. Other doors conceal storage for clothes and shoes. Everything is hidden, leaving the bed in stately isolation.

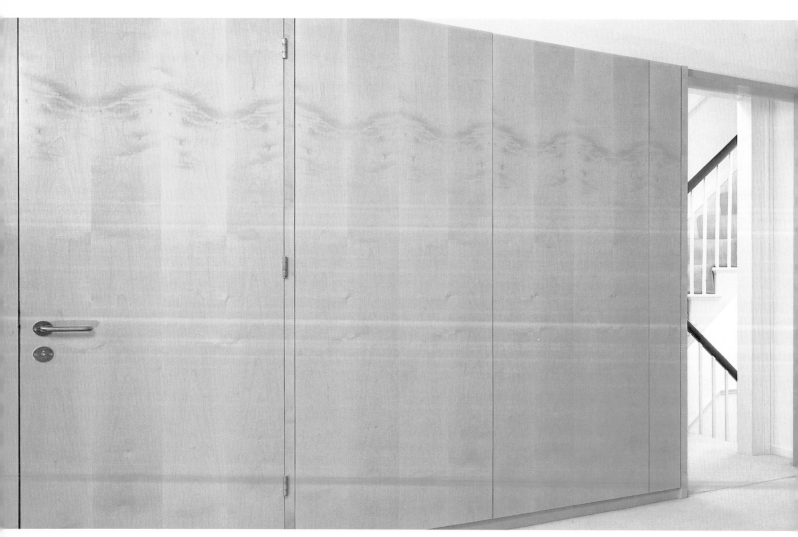

Left: This long, narrow room doubles as a home office and a spare bedroom. It has cupboards at each end and a sitting area in the middle. At one end the cupboards contain the office, at the other clothes. The sofa opens out into a bed when required.

A Shaker kitchen (above) has a place for everything. Each drawer is the right size for the objects or produce stored within. If you have many small drawers, you lose a little storage space because of the division.

An old haberdasher's cabinet (left) makes a wonderful storage unit for paints, bubbles, and modeling clay in a child's bedroom. Originally, it displayed gloves and ribbons; now the glass-fronted cupboards allow you to see exactly what is within.

Every genuine farmhouse kitchen, and many others besides, has a generous cupboard that opens its arms to a huge quantity of china, glass, and anything else that will fit into its various recesses. The paintwork on this one is charmingly distressed.

85

*Right: A severely minimalist bedroom,
the only color being the stripes on the bed
linen. To achieve a look that is this pure
you need large areas of fitted cupboard to
contain all your possessions. Even then,
you need to be selective about what you
keep and accumulate further.*

This minimalist kitchen (left) has
quantities of storage behind the folding
doors of floor-to-ceiling cupboards. On the
opposite wall is a stone sink and a small
stovetop. There is no oven. A microwave,
the fridge, and everything else is hidden in
the cupboards.

This bedroom (right) is enlivened by the
cupboards being painted a delicate shade
of duck-egg blue, a color that is continued
onto the ceiling. There is no furniture in
the room other than the bed.

Cupboards, drawers, and shelves are built into the wall that divides the dining room (far left) from the kitchen beyond. This clever arrangement has the double effect of providing copious storage for china and glass while creating a spacious entrance to the reception room. A bathroom (left) with a wall of small cupboards, each with a slightly overlapping lift-up door. Drawers and cupboards (below and below left) in different finishes have a contemporary look, enhanced by the stainless steel handles.

A large storage unit, with cupboards above and drawers below, that is invaluable in any kitchen. It takes up a lot of room, but you can store substantial quantities of kitchenware in it as well as all the clutter of foil, food wrap, spare tea towels, and other kitchen linen.

FREESTANDING FURNITURE

GOOD-QUALITY FREESTANDING CUPBOARDS, wardrobes, and chests of drawers, whether antique or modern, are expensive. You are, after all, buying something that has been carefully designed and crafted with skill, using materials that will last. The expense may alarm you into thinking that the fitted alternative is better. It may be, but if you find a piece of furniture that gives you pleasure to look at and supplies the storage you need, you will find it is an investment. It will pay you back with good service and comfortable companionship over many years.

Moreover, not all freestanding storage furniture is conventional in appearance – far from it. Whether your style is industrial chic, classic contemporary, or colorful bohemian, you will be able to find storage that matches. Wire-mesh school lockers, high-sided industrial units with wheels, scaffolding-like clamped racking systems, filing cabinets, old wooden shop fittings ... the possibilities are almost endless. Sources include not only shops, junk emporiums, and auction rooms, but also secondhand office stores and catalogs of industrial and laboratory goods.

Contemporary furniture and product designers have become champions of storage. Modules and units that you fit together to make any configuration of shelves and cupboards are made in a huge variety of styles and materials, from traditional fine woods to polished concrete to cardboard. Wire mesh, fiberglass, molded plastic, and plywood have also found favor again. These were all materials popular with influential furniture designers of the 1950s, like Ray and Charles Eames and Arne Jacobsen.

Among the most intriguing free-standing cupboards is Ubald Klug's "Shell." Closed, this looks like an up-ended, sleek black trunk of the type carried about the world by previous centuries' empire builders. Inside, it can be finished to fulfill the function of wardrobe or mobile office or even a kitchen – ideal for a very small or minimalist interior.

CUSTOMIZING CHEAP FURNITURE

ACHEAPER OPTION is to buy mass-produced or junk-shop furniture and customize it, outside and in. This involves some effort on your part, as well as exercising your imagination. Customizing can be as simple as changing the handles or adding a coat

of paint (having first sandpapered and primed). Or the answer may be to change the legs
or add a simple architrave around the top in the case of a wardrobe or tall cupboard.
Inside, you may want to add shelves or hooks, or replace the center panels of the doors
with fabric, wire mesh, or glass.

More drastic customization can involve sawing up two or more pieces of cheap
furniture and attaching the best parts to each other to make a completely "new" item.
Take an old flat-fronted dressing table with drawers, for example, one that has lost its
mirror and been coated with dark varnish that is now scratched and worn. Saw off the
wings or shelves and mirror supports, then place on top of the drawers a cupboard of
similar or slightly smaller base dimensions. Cut out a shaped molding from MDF or other
smooth board to add a flourish to the top, and screw all the separate parts together
securely. Once the whole has been sandpapered, primed, painted with several coats, and
had matching handles or knobs attached to all the relevant places, you will have a
magnificent if eccentric piece of furniture that will provide you with copious storage for
years to come.

BUILT-IN
FURNITURE

THE CONSIDERABLE ADVANTAGES that built-in cupboards and drawers have over
freestanding ones is that they make maximum possible use of the available space,
and that the arrangement of drawers, shelves, and rails inside can be designed to match
your needs. They can also be used to make sense of awkward corners or strangely shaped
rooms, by concealing them or squaring them off.

If you build your own fitted cupboards, look in a home supply or renovation cata-
log for ready-made doors to help make your job easier. Mass-produced room doors,
plain or paneled, can also provide a shortcut to a handsome finished cupboard or
wardrobe.

Remember, though, that cupboards do not have to be built squarely onto the wall —
that is, so that the doors at the front are parallel with the wall behind. You can have
your cupboards built at an angle. This means that they are deeper at one end than the
other, so arrange the contents accordingly. There are various possible reasons why you
might want to have angled cupboards. One is in order to lead the eye into another
area, whereas square-on cupboards would stop the eye dead, creating a visual barrier.
Another reason is to give you more storage when, for example, the room is an unusual

*Before and after (above). If you want to
be able to find something readily, and in
good condition, there is no alternative to
keeping the inside of your closets tidy.
Arrange your clothes by kind, color,
length, and type.*

A dressing area has been created by giving part of the bedroom over to a walk-through closet, through which you reach the bathroom.

A sumptuous dressing room. The doors of the wardrobes are lined with gathered fabric. A similar effect could be reproduced by taking the center panels out of used panel doors.

shape, narrower at one end than another, or where there is a room door near one end of the cupboards.

If you build fitted cupboards that are at an angle, there is one technical detail to be aware of. When cupboards are square-on, the doors usually open 90 degrees, or at right angles, to the cupboard and the wall behind. When the cupboard front is at an angle, you still probably want the doors to open 90 degrees to the wall. But in order to do this, the doors with hinges on the deeper side of the cupboard have to be able to swing more than this in relation to the front of the cupboard. In a kitchen, this might require special hinges, a point that you should make to your carpenter or cabinetmaker if he or she has not already noticed it.

CUPBOARD FRONTS

A BUILT-IN WARDROBE or cupboard does not have to have conventional molded-timber doors. A gathered curtain, either one that matches other fabric or colors in the room, or one on which you have painted a special pattern or design, can be hung across the front of a wardrobe on a track or, more decorative, a pole. Allow extra length in the pole to enable you to pull the curtain completely clear of the storage space so you can see inside and freely access the contents.

Creating your own design on a curtain is less complicated than it might seem. All you need is a design on paper, some home-craft fabric paints or pens, an iron or oven to set the colors, and a dash of confidence and enthusiasm. Lay the fabric flat onto newspaper (absorbent) with plastic sheeting (nonabsorbent) underneath. Draw or paint the design, which could be inspired by a detail or feature elsewhere in the room, and set it according to the manufacturer's instructions.

The simplest gathered curtain has a slot heading: a channel along the top (created by turning the fabric over by an inch or so and sewing it) through which you slot the pole. If the curtain is lightweight, the pole could simply be a piece of doweling, a bamboo cane, or a length of copper plumbing pipe.

A flat curtain takes up less space than a gathered one and can fit just as well into a cool, minimalist interior as a warm, cozy one, depending on the fabric and color that you use. Make sure that the curtain is set well back from the contents, so that they do not nudge it and spoil the flat, smooth look. Weight the bottom of the curtain to help keep it flat, either with ribbon weights or with a piece of wood run through the bottom. The latter is suitable only for narrow curtains (of which you could have several across the front of a wide cupboard) and should be removable so that you can wash the curtain.

Another clever wardrobe front can be constructed with MDF and bamboo shades. Cut an interestingly shaped frame for the wardrobe from MDF, paint it, and hang two or three tall, fairly narrow shades behind it on track so that they slide across the front. Sliding doors have the advantage of taking up no extra space, unlike swinging doors, which need space into which to open. The disadvantage of sliding doors is that you cannot see and have access to the entire cupboard at one time.

Mirrored wardrobe doors in a bedroom create an illusion of greater space, but will reflect and double the appearance of any untidiness in the room, and you will constantly see yourself when you may not feel ready to face the world. Limiting mirrors to a looking glass on the wall or on your dressing table gives you the choice of being selective with your reflection.

ORGANIZING YOUR WARDROBE

ORGANIZING YOUR WARDROBE is one of the great tests of your commitment to transforming your life through storage. It is relatively easy and very satisfying to arrange your clothes and shoes properly for the first time (or the first time in a long while). Maintaining the organization is the real proof that you are converted.

Take everything out of the wardrobe or closet and clean the inside thoroughly. Look at all your clothes carefully. Be realistic. If you have not worn something for five years, or even two, are you ever likely to wear it again? If you think you might, archive the garment or footwear in an old suitcase or chest of drawers in the attic and see if you can live without it. If you decide to part with it, dispose of it by giving it away, selling it, or in one of the other ways described in Chapter Two, page 22. Also, pack away clothes that are out of season.

Once you have reduced the quantity of your clothing in this way, sort the remaining garments. Invest in a collection of slim hangers of similar design to each other rather than using wire coat hangers, so that they look smart and orderly on the pole. Because you have reduced their number, each garment should have more space in which to hang, so that it is not squashed by its neighbor.

Sort your clothes according to length, and within each range sort them by color. Hang the longest at one end of your wardrobe and so on until the shortest. Besides looking good, this arrangement will help you find what you want when you want it, quickly and without stress.

Household linen stored in a cupboard with glass doors has to be tidily arranged, but the advantage is that you can see at a glance what is where. You can also place your prettiest pieces in positions where they will be seen for everyone to enjoy.

A shoe hanger made of see-through plastic with pockets, into each of which you place one shoe. Separate pockets prevent shoes from rubbing against each other, and you can see at a glance exactly where each pair is stored.

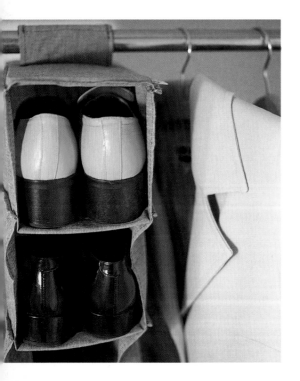

This type of shoe hanger hangs from a closet pole. It has compartments, each the size of a shoe box, into which you slot a pair of shoes. If you buy a shoe hanger made of pale fabric, check that it is washable.

Organizing your wardrobe should free a considerable amount of space beneath, mainly for footwear. If your shoes and boots are in a jumble, separate them into pairs. Clean them, condition and polish them as appropriate, and fit them with shoe trees or, at the least, crumpled tissue paper to help them keep their shape. Replace them in clearly labeled boxes or bags (see Chapter Six, page 58) on shelves or in racks.

Alternative ways of storing shoes include displaying them on open racks in the bottom of the wardrobe, and slotting them into the pockets of a canvas or plastic shoe hanger. Check that any shoe hanger you buy is washable, especially if it is made of cloth in white or natural, which will become dirty in due course. Wire baskets that slide into a metal frame, creating a stack of drawers, offer another useful method of storing shoes in a wardrobe.

If you share your closet space with another person, consider how the space is arranged. Could it be better organized by hanging all your and his or her short garments in one place, for example, and all your long ones in a different area? Closet systems are available that will make the most of available closet space. If you have more clothes and shoes, does he or she have more computer and office equipment elsewhere in the home? Could these needs for space be balanced amicably?

DRAWERS

DRAWERS HAVE THE ADVANTAGE over shelves in that they may be pulled out so you can see the items at the back equally as well as the ones at the front. Whether in the kitchen or the bedroom, drawers prevent things from "disappearing," never to be seen again (or not until they are wildly out of date). Shallow drawers, or drawers that are no deeper than they need be, are better than deep ones. Transparent drawers, made from wire or acrylic, for example, also help prevent things from sinking without trace.

A simple item like this honeycomb drawer organizer (below) can help you transform the muddle of a drawer like this (left) into perfect order.

The steps towards organizing your drawers are the same as for cupboards. Empty everything out and take a dispassionate look at each item. When you have decided what to keep, sort these things into types and colors. Make each item separate – each pair of socks folded together, for example, and each sweater folded neatly so that the arms do not trail about. Sweaters and other bulky items should be folded so that they exactly fit the depth of the drawer from back to front, rather than lying along the drawer. This will make it easier to see what you want at a glance.

Replace your clothes and other possessions carefully and without squashing them into the drawers, thinking about the most suitable position for each type or item. You may want to divide your drawers into sections for different kinds of things, or even for individual items like pairs of socks. Drawer organizers can be bought to make this an easy task. Beware of over-organizing yourself, however. You want your new-found storage intelligence to set you free, not make a slave of you.

IDEA BOX

CUPBOARDS AND DRAWERS FOR STORAGE INCLUDE:

* Antique furniture

* Fine modern furniture

* Customized cheap furniture

* Flat built-in storage

* Angled built-in storage

* Fitted cupboards with curtains, blinds, or doors

TIPS ON ORGANIZING YOUR WARDROBE

* Take everything out.

* Give/throw/pack away things you don't want or don't wear.

* Make sure the rest is clean and in good condition.

* Choose identical slim hangers.

* Hang clothes according to length and color.

* Apportion space amicably.

* Clean and condition your footwear.

* Replace shoes in boxes/bags/racks/pockets.

* Fold sweaters, etc., neatly to fit drawers.

* Lay clothes in drawers arranged according to color.

* Don't squash your clothes together – give them room to breathe.

THE ULTIMATE KITCHEN

Opposite: The modern equivalent of the large kitchen cupboard: tall sliding doors with Japanese-style gauzy panels hide shelves laden with the thousand things needed in a contemporary living kitchen.

Left: The tower block in the middle of the kitchen looks like a piece of sculpture. In fact, its many cupboards house almost everything required in a kitchen, apart from the sink, which can be seen beyond.

O F ALL THE ROOMS IN THE HOUSE, the one in which the largest number of your possessions is stored is probably the kitchen. Once the domain of farmers' wives and, in wealthier households, of servants, the kitchen is now quite often the most-used room, the place where most family activities occur and where friends gather.

The postmodern kitchen, as much as the farmhouse kitchen of country lore, has to earn its living by being all things to all people in the household.

For children it is a place for messy activities like painting, model making, and clay sculpture, not to mention "helping" with food preparation and cooking. The kitchen is also a place for older children to do their homework in a companionable setting.

It is the room to which visitors automatically gravitate, perhaps asking "Can I do anything to help?", or just to share a freshly brewed cup of coffee during a break between jobs.

On a chilly winter morning, it is often the first room to get really warm; on a summer's evening after a hot, humid day, it offers a cool refuge from the heat. Influenced by the professional restaurant kitchen and by interest in the cooking techniques of many countries, the contemporary kitchen is home to a thrilling range of gadgets, implements, ingredients, and basic cookware, not to mention the china, glass, and cutlery with which we eat and drink the resulting exotic creations.

The ultimate kitchen of our dreams has everything that is needed, everything at hand, everything organized and beautiful. Everything in perfect order.

The inspiration for this kitchen storage with sensually curved flip-up doors came from automotive technology, specifically Lamborghini's "gull-wing" doors, says their designer Martin Lee. This entire house was decorated as a showcase for contemporary design in the home.

This side of the kitchen (right) is only half of a long island unit attached to the white wall at the end. On the other side, under the spacious worktop, are cupboards that conceal the television, music system, telephone directories, and other living room clutter. Opposite is a well-planned small kitchen.

This kitchen (above) is in an immaculate apartment owned and lived in by one tidy person. Everything has a place, and everything is in its place, in the kitchen as elsewhere. The wooden block for storing knives has been hooked onto the rail, from which hang various small stainless steel utensils. There is a similar arrangement (right) in this bustling family kitchen, but here, pans and colanders are hung from a rail suspended by chain from the ceiling.

A Shaker-style kitchen (left) complete with the appropriate table and chairs. Once again, peg rails make a significant contribution to storage arrangements.

A magnificent array of cookware (right) hanging from a rail under a shelf in a large family kitchen. Lids are stored on top of the shelf, and below the counter is the electric stove, which is used in summer. This kitchen also has an English gas stove (opposite page).

The rack suspended from the ceiling over a countertop, or kitchen island, is a useful way of storing attractive items for instant access. Such a rack could be made from wood, as here, or metal.

THE WORK AREA

HOW YOU ORGANIZE YOUR STORAGE will depend to some extent on the shape and layout of your kitchen. The four classic kitchen arrangements are the U-shape, the galley, the L-shape, and the island. The U-shape has work surface on three sides; the galley has a counter along one or both long side(s) of a rectangle. The L-shape is exactly that, on two sides at right angles to each other. An island configuration is a variation on the L, with a block of work surface with storage beneath and sometimes a stove top or sink in the crook of the L-shape.

Whatever the floor plan, there are certain guidelines that make a kitchen safer and more efficient. One is to have a flat, heatproof surface immediately to at least one side of the stove, so that you do not need to walk anywhere holding something that is scalding hot. Another is not to have cupboard doors opening into a throughway, where people walk to get to the table or door. Yet another is to have the dishwasher just to one side of a sink, and not creating a blockage when the door is opened down.

One "rule" about which there is disagreement is whether your everyday china and glass should be stored close to the dishwasher or to the table where it is used. The latter arrangement makes setting the table quicker and easier, but the former makes emptying the dishwasher less tiresome. Clearly this is a matter of personal preference, but the following questions may help you make a decision. Which is the more interesting job? And who is most likely to be doing each task? If you believe that emptying the dishwasher is one of the least exciting requirements of running a kitchen, and that it is as likely to be someone else setting the table as you yourself, store the china near the machine.

The usual sequence of machinery is refrigerator or refrigerator/freezer, stove, sink, dishwasher, with the microwave near the stove. If you are planning a kitchen from scratch, draw it on paper first. Better still, make cutout shapes representing your various pieces of machinery, units and/or furniture and move them around until you are satisfied.

Mass-produced kitchen units are basically boxes in regular sizes, onto which you put doors and a work surface. The height of a base unit is generally 36 inches, the depth around 24 inches. Widths are more varied: 12 inches, 20 inches, 24 inches, and 36 inches. There are also corner units, and some ranges have special pieces like tray stores, wine racks, and curved end units. These sizes were determined at some time in the past as being appropriate to a person of average height. Very few of us are average, however, and you might prefer to have a kitchen that fits you.

Standard units can be cut down or, even better for storage, raised up on a custom-made plinth so that you do not have to stoop, if you are taller than "average." Have drawers set into the plinth for added storage space. Your work surface can also be made deeper than usual from back to front. This is a clever ruse to give you more counter area if there is only limited space for your working area lengthwise along the wall. Have your kitchen custom built by a cabinetmaker (or make it yourself), and your taller, deeper units will also give you plenty of extra storage space beneath the counter.

Wall-mounted units are generally 12 inches deep and vary in height from 3 to 4 feet. With a high ceiling, you could have two layers of cupboards on the walls, or have custom-made cupboards that reach to the ceiling to give you additional storage space.

Once the plan of your kitchen is established, categorize all the storage space it offers into three access categories: primary, secondary, and tertiary. Primary storage includes space on the work surface itself, immediately below it and immediately above – places that you can reach instantly without having to bend or stretch. Secondary storage includes areas lower down and higher up, but near the center of activity, the stove/refrigerator/sink zone. Tertiary storage is across the other side of the room, in the pantry, and any other place to which you have to walk more than a couple of steps, or for access to which you need a stepladder.

Primary storage is obviously for the things you use most often, secondary and tertiary being similarly allocated according to frequency of use. If you have small children, or regular small visitors, this may also influence where you keep certain things.

The other side of the kitchen on the opposite page, this time showing the gas stove and surround. There should always be a flat, preferably heatproof surface next to at least one side of a stove, so that you do not have to walk across the room carrying something that is scalding hot, with the consequent danger to yourself and others.

COOKING

IN GENERAL (but not always, as with the dishwasher) it is helpful to store things near where they are used. This makes for speed and a relaxed working environment. When you need a knife and a board for chopping, they are there beside you. When you want your favorite wok and wooden spatula, there they are. Keep the counter free of all but the most often used equipment, to leave space to work.

Shelves (above) made of stainless steel give a kitchen a professional, industrial appearance. Near the stove, things stored on open shelves may acquire a film of grease, even if you have an exhaust hood.

A simple kitchen table with extending leaves (above) has been given a new lease on life with a new metal top, which ties in visually with the row of enamel pans stored hung in a row above.

If you use a food processor or other heavy appliance regularly, keep it easily to hand either on the work surface or in a cupboard on a mixer platform. This swings up from the cupboard beneath and clicks into place level with the countertop. The advantage of this is that it is concealed when not in use, but can be pulled out effortlessly when it is needed. The disadvantage is that the appliance and platform take up a large part of the cupboard.

Find places close to the center of activity for any other such appliance that you regularly use, such as a blender or heavy-duty mixer. Think about the requirements of each machine and plan accordingly. A coffee grinder, for example, ideally should be near the coffee beans, the coffee maker, the kettle, and/or the sink. The heavy-duty mixer should be near the flour canister and pastry board. These ideals cannot always be fulfilled, but by thinking about how and how often you use the appliances, you can supply at least some.

Sharp knives can be kept in a wooden block on the work surface, or on the wall on a magnetic strip, or in a knife holder in a drawer. Other frequently used cooking implements can be stored in a jar or drawer near the stove. Beware of your implement drawer becoming a hopeless mess. Instead, install dividers and keep like with like. Two methods of maximizing space in your drawer are the sliding insert and the not-used-often box.

The sliding insert is a shallow tray that is the same width but only half or less the depth of the drawer. It slides backwards and forwards on runners across the top of the drawer's other contents, giving you half as much storage again. The not-used-often box is an open-top box kept in a tertiary position, where you leave kitchen tools, like a cherry stoner or melon baller, that you use only very occasionally or seasonally. It provides backup while keeping everything orderly.

Pans can look magnificent, or a mess. If you have sets of stainless steel, enamel, or copper pans, keep them on display, hiding less attractive cookware in a cupboard. You can range the set on a shelf near the stove, in a cupboard or dresser bottom with glass doors, or on a pan stand. This is a helpful structure, available in various finishes and styles, that consists of a series of round or square shelves, one above the other, graduated in size with the largest at the bottom. You store one pan on each shelf. The beauty of the pan stand is that it can make use of a corner that might otherwise stand empty.

Another way of storing pans and other utensils is to hang them up near the cooking area, from a beam or rack – assuming that your kitchen ceiling is sufficiently high. This has the dual effect of using space for storage that would otherwise be thin air, and of storing the items so that they are instantly at hand. It is suitable only for things of light to medium weight, obviously: small and medium pans, sieves, steamers and colanders, and ladles.

An under-counter corner cupboard is a good place to store pans, because a two-tier carousel can be installed that will swing out, making use of what can be an inaccessible space. In general, though, beware of fitting drawers of any sort inside a cupboard, as you create work for yourself (getting at the stuff is a two-stage process) and the drawer may knock against the door annoyingly when you pull it out.

Metal things such as pan lids, cake pans, roasting pans, and baking sheets quickly fill a large amount of space, and they can become jumbled. Separate them into those that are fairly flat and those that are not. The fairly flat items such as baking sheets, wire racks, splatter guards, and pan lids can be stood upright or on their sides, like books, in a deep drawer or in a cupboard. A wire rack may help keep them from falling over. Stack the rest in a deep drawer or cupboard, keeping like with like. Don't be afraid to divide these objects into those used frequently and others – as always, store the ones you use least often in a tertiary position.

Cooking ingredients such as oils (except some nut oils, which go rancid relatively quickly and should be kept in the refrigerator), vinegars, soy and fish sauces, salt and pepper, kept on a shelf to one side of the stove, will make an attractive sight. Alternatively, store them in a cupboard close by, or in a bottle basket of the type designed for picnics, which can be kept elsewhere in the room and carried to the cooking area when needed.

Herbs and spices are easily accessible stored in a spice rack, and you can see at a glance if they are running out. In a cupboard, the least-used ones tend to disappear to the back where they clutter the space and go stale, forgotten. To prevent this happening, either use a turntable, or keep them in alphabetical order in a wire or plastic box so that you can pull the whole lot out.

Kitchens with cabinets above and below make the best possible use of space. This one has smart white knobs on moss green doors, which gives the room a country feel.

EATING

STORE YOUR CHINA AND GLASS so that it is convenient and makes a fine display, on open shelves, in a hutch, or in cupboards with glass or wire-mesh door panels. (For more on this, see Chapter Seven, page 70.) In order for it to look interesting rather than a jumble, have only china and glass, with a strong visual link on display. Put the rest in a cupboard where it won't be seen. Unifying elements could be color, pattern, or period, or it could all be the work of one pottery, potter, or glassmaker.

Cup hooks screwed into the underside of shelves create up storage for mugs and jugs. The hooks come in various sizes to support even large pieces of china, provided the shelf is strong enough. They can also be screwed into beams and the sides of cupboards to provide storage space where there was none before.

*Three ways of storing cutlery: in a
wooden box (bottom), in a wicker basket
(middle), and standing upright in three
separate but similar terra-cotta flower pots.
In each case, the knives, forks, and spoons
are separated. The flowerpots are witty
because the cutlery stands up in them like
the stalks or fronds of real plants.*

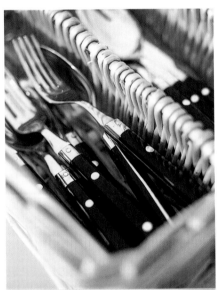

Cutlery can be stored in a wide, flat drawer with dividers, or in a shallow box or a
divided carrier that can easily be brought to the table for laying. The latter solution neatly
solves the problem of whether to keep cutlery near the dishwasher or near the table.

If you need a place for snacks and feeding children, as opposed to a table for formal
meals, one way of achieving this and using space cleverly is to have cupboards beneath
and extend the work surface beyond the back of them so that you can fit your knees
underneath on the other side. This way you have extra counter space when there is no
meal in progress, and the (extra-deep) eating area demands only a little additional space
beyond the cupboards.

FRESH FOOD

MOST FRESH FOOD is kept in the refrigerator (raw meat in the bottom, away from
cooked meat). You can store root vegetables other than potatoes in the
refrigerator, but if they take up too much room you can keep them just as well in the
dark in a basket, rack, or drawer with your potatoes. The truly ultimate dream kitchen has
separately operated refrigerated and dehumidified drawers (as opposed to drawers in
the refrigerator) for vegetables, bread, and so on, but this rather an expensive option
for most people.

A simple and inexpensive alternative is to create a ventilated drawer in your existing
kitchen. This should be fairly deep – remember that you are storing bags of potatoes and
onions in it – and have runners that are strong enough to take the weight. Drill ventilation
holes at intervals along the sides of your bottom kitchen drawer, and perhaps some along
the front if this can be done neatly. Set a rack or racks in the bottom of the drawer (wire
racks will do) to allow air under the vegetables, and use it regularly to ensure good air
circulation. In a temperate atmosphere, this should be sufficient to store your vegetables
in good order.

Vegetables (left) need to be cool and well aired to stay fresh. A colorful plastic vegetable bin like this could be used for various storage functions in different rooms in the house. Spices look pretty in matching jars (right), as do herbs and spices in test tubes supported by their own little rack (below).

THE PANTRY

THE PANTRY is for canned and packaged food, dry goods such as flour for baking, and back-up stores of staples like salt and olive oil. The ultimate pantry is a walk-in butler's pantry, with a marble or slate slab for storing cooked or prepared food in anticipation of a meal or party, and shelves up the walls. Most of us have to make do with a cupboard or a couple of drawers.

You might not think of a drawer as a place to store food, but it is ideal in that you can pull it out and see right to the back at a glance. If you are having a kitchen built for you, measure your supplies and have drawers made to fit – one for cans and jams, perhaps, and a deeper one below for larger packages and jars. Things you use less than often, such as birthday cake candles and party supplies, can go in a tertiary position.

If you do keep your pantry goods in a cupboard, there is an easy way of keeping things from disappearing to the back. Simply cut a U shape out of the middle of the front of each shelf. You lose a little surface area, but gain greatly in accessibility. Moreover, if the cupboard is tall, you can hang a hook for aprons or string bags on the middle of the inside of the cupboard door – there is now space for them to hang down.

WINE AND DRINKS

IF POSSIBLE, keep bottles of wine and other drinks elsewhere, apart from the kinds that you consume regularly. Once you start to store drinks in the kitchen, they can quickly demand a large amount of space. A cellar or outbuilding is ideal, if you are lucky enough to have one, and more likely to offer a suitable temperature for storing wine, in particular (see Chapter Twelve, page 146, for more about wine cellars).

This drying/storage rack suspended from the ceiling is an inspiration. It uses space that might otherwise be wasted, yet leaves the entire countertop free. It provides visible storage for beautiful household china (what is more thrilling than rows of simple white plates?) as well as a practical way of drying wet dishes without occupying precious worktop space. It also acts as a screen between the kitchen and dining areas, enabling the cook to join in conversation, and guests or family to enjoy the sounds and smells of delicious cooking, at the same time acting as a screen to hide the mess and clutter of food preparation.

DISH WASHING

THE CLUTTER OF DISH SOAP, scouring pads, hand cream, brushes, and so on is often invisible to the person who runs the kitchen and sees them all the time. To give you more space, however, and to improve the appearance of your sink area, simply store them in the cupboard beneath with other cleaning requirements, like an extra dishpan for washing vegetables and the dishwasher powder.

If your standard unit cupboard has a shelf that prevents you from fitting in larger items, you can simply cut all or part of it away.

TRASH

WHERE AND HOW YOU STORE your kitchen trash is a surprisingly complex issue. There are many strongly held views on the subject – yours may be among them. If you are in doubt, however, here are some of the options.

The simplest and least ecologically friendly system is to have a large bin into which you put all kitchen trash and which you empty regularly. Most people, however, separate at least some of their trash for recycling.

If you have a comprehensive recycling system, some of it is better housed in another room, such as a utility room or downstairs cloakroom if you have one, a basement or garage, or even in a cupboard under the stairs.

A recycling system takes up space, and the items, once placed there, are not used again (except for jars and bottles to be reused). The following can be separated and recycled separately:

- glass for disposal
- glass jars and bottles for reuse
- plastic containers and bags for disposal
- plastic and other containers, empty toilet paper rolls, and anything that your own or other children make into models
- paper and cardboard
- steel cans

- aluminum foil
- aluminum cans
- textiles (old tea towels and dishcloths, as well as clothes)
- books (including hopelessly outdated cookbooks)
- uncooked vegetable matter for compost
- shoes (in pairs)

Doors open to reveal a trash can on the right and a free-wheeling drying rack on the left. The can is concealed below the work surface, where an ingenious chute arrangement allows the cook to discard trash into it without removing it from the cupboard. The cupboard is by the front door for quick disposal, avoiding mess.

Laundry hampers (below) are no longer necessarily wicker or white plastic. This is an example of the new generation of utilitarian and colorful household wares. In a small apartment, the washing machine may be in a room just off the kitchen.

Some people save their leftover food scraps to make compost. They may keep a small bin or lidded bucket actually in the kitchen for gathering compost materials pending a trip to the compost heap, or prefer to walk a few steps from the house to a concealed container, in order to avoid smells in the kitchen. A small container in the kitchen will not smell, however, if you empty it regularly. A compost heap near the house will smell, in summer. Most people, whether in city, country, or suburbs, have a built-in garbage disposal for such scraps, or simply throw them out along with other trash.

A hotly debated subject is the type and size of the ideal trash can. Some people prefer their can concealed in a kitchen cupboard, because it is neater. There are several types of these:

- A small plastic bag is gripped by a lidded clip on the back of the cupboard door. You simply release the bag when it is full and take it to the outdoor trash can. The disadvantage of this is that it will not take trash that is heavier than lightweight (the bag drops out of the clip), and it is small (advocates of the small trash can consider this an advantage).

- A small trash can kept on the floor of the cupboard; when you open the door a pulley lifts the lid.
- The entire cupboard door tilts forward (hinged at the bottom) to reveal a full-size trash container or bag clipped in place, which also tilts.

Other people prefer a trash can that is freestanding, for two main reasons: A built-in can occupies valuable storage space; and, second, a freestanding can is more versatile because you can carry it to the place where the trash has been created and simply sweep it in off

A slip of a cupboard exactly fits the width of the iron and the height of the ironing board. A rack for drying laundry is invaluable. This one has round bars, which can turn and drop laundry on the floor; those with bars that have a rectangular profile are preferable.

the work surface. The difficulty is to find a can that conceals the plastic bag. Alternatively, some cans have an inner can or liner that you empty, avoiding the need for plastic bags. This solution is ideal if the only things which go into your trash can are dry goods that cannot be recycled, otherwise you will have to wash the liner each time you empty the can. Depending on your area, some garbage collectors will not accept trash unless it is in bags.

There is also a debate about the size of can ideal for storing kitchen trash. Advocates of the small bin say that they don't want a bigger one because they don't want trash to sit and smell. This may hold true in a small household, with only one or two people. In a larger one, a small can will often be full to overflowing and, of course, you can empty a large can as often as a small one if you want to.

OTHER THINGS

When planning your ultimate kitchen, do not forget to include ample storage space for the following important items:

- chopping boards, cheese boards, pastry board or marble, carving board

- place mats

- napkins and napkin rings

- aluminum foil, plastic wrap, baking parchment, sandwich bags, freezer bags, etc.

- ties, string, rubber bands, labels

- paper towels, paper napkins

- plastic trash bags

- plastic boxes and lids for the freezer, picnics, lunches

- Other types of sealed containers such as cans or small glass storage jars for miscellaneous items such as tea bags, pasta, dried beans, etc.

- trays – they are invaluable and take up more space than you think, depending on how high the sides are raised

- tea towels and oven mitts or hot pads currently in use

- clean tea towels and oven mitts/ hot pads

- aprons

- keys in regular use

- keys used rarely

- notices

- the ongoing shopping list and pen

- information needed near the telephone, such as telephone directories, paper and pen for taking messages, shopping information

- emergency information, perhaps including a first-aid book

- a small fire extinguisher

This is most people's dream storage: a walk-in area for stacks of china, glass, mixing and serving bowls, baskets, ice bucket, and plentiful stocks of wine.

The shelving is simple and utilitarian, although it would not disgrace the kitchen proper. It is a design easily copied by a local carpenter.

It is always useful to have a ready supply of plastic and paper bags from supermarkets and other shops. Possible storage solutions for these include a drawer devoted to them in a communal room, such as the kitchen – because, no doubt, every member of the family will need one from time to time.

Alternatively, a bag for bags hanging on a hook positioned on the back of a door will keep them tidily stored but accessible. Though fairly practical, this solution is not aesthetically pleasing.

Another neat solution to this storage problem is a tubular container, bought or made, through the top of which you add a folded bag, and from the bottom of which you draw the next bag. The advantage of the latter system over the others is that it compacts the bags so that they take up less room; the disadvantage is that you can't rummage for a bag of the size and type that you need, as you can with the other systems.

Plastic containers such as Tupperware are useful for all sorts of purposes, especially in a family home, but they can be a nuisance to store until needed. If you do not have a deep bottom drawer where you can keep them in the kitchen itself, consider storing them in a large net bag (so you can see what is there) in your basement, garage, or utility room.

IDEA BOX

STORAGE TIPS FOR THE ULTIMATE KITCHEN

* Plan storage for your whole kitchen using lists, drawings, cutouts.

* Keep it safe: remember children.

* Create more storage space by raising and customizing units, having extra wall cupboards, or having your kitchen custom built.

* In general, store things near where they are used.

* Keep only the most frequently used items on the work surface.

* Knives: Store them in a block or on a magnetic strip to keep them handy and sharp.

* Utensils 1: Store the most often used in a jar or divided drawer, like with like.

* Utensils 2: Keep those used less frequently in a "not-used-often box" away from prime storage area.

* Store flat items like baking sheets upright.

* Display sets of pans, china, glass.

* Keep cutlery in a divided box to carry to the table for setting.

* Use drawers for keeping dry goods and cans.

* Store drinks elsewhere, except for a few kinds most often used.

* Store dishwashing liquid, etc., out of sight.

STORING THE FAMILY

The child in this photograph (left) is in an ingeniously devised "castle," a raised play area that has a balustrade all the way around and is entirely visible from the other areas of the kitchen.

In the same house, a huge hamper acts as a toy box. This is a family-friendly house, arranged so that not only the children but also the adults have areas that are exclusively theirs.

A CCORDING TO AN OLD ADAGE, "You can't have too much storage space." In a family home this could be translated into "You never seem to have sufficient storage space." The problem of storing the family is an endless one. The solution, as so often with storage problems, is to tackle it from several directions at the same time.

When you are single, storage may be an irritant but it is rarely a problem. When you set up house with another person, you make space for that person (or vice versa) by moving things around and putting some of them in boxes in the attic. When you start a family, you are too busy and tired to think about anything much at all, let alone the question of storage.

To make matters worse, everyone you know showers you with toys, presents, equipment, and furniture to supplement the pieces you have already acquired. Before you know it, the problem has crept up on you and goes "Boo!" in your face every time you search for a place to put a new possession. Perfect order seems as distant and inaccessible as the moon.

Keep calm, and look for new places to store things: up storage that will make use of under-exploited wall space, for example. Be realistic – broken toys and jigsaw puzzles with half the pieces missing are rarely worth keeping unless they have a very special sentimental value of some sort.

Be organized. Set up workable systems, label them clearly and cheerfully, then train your family to use them.

A drawstring bag (above) made in jolly
red and yellow gingham checks hangs from
the cupboard door knob. Bags like this
are useful for storing one type of item or
toy: cotton handkerchiefs, for example,
or Lego pieces.

Stacking plastic crates (right) that have
one side open are as useful for storing toys
in the nursery as they are for vegetables in
the kitchen. Access is immediate, which is
not the case with ordinary stacking crates.
Baskets, bags, and miniature suitcases are
beloved by children for storing treasures.

An eye-catching cupboard (left) in the
same children's bedroom. If the storage is
colorful and attractive, children are more
likely to use it. It should also be accessible;
this cupboard, positioned on the wall,
would be a good place to store delicate or
messy things away from little fingers.

Above: The same child's bedroom as opposite, showing how raising the mattress onto a platform has liberated plenty of floor space beneath for storage of toys as well as for playing. The shelves on the far wall have a deep drawer in the bottom and enough height above this to stand a small dollhouse where it is off the floor but nonetheless accessible to the child.

Opposite: A delightfully simple idea: a paper screen with cut-out window and flowers painted along the bottom transform the under-bed area into a playhouse in this child's bedroom. The shelves on the wall opposite are used for storing many much-loved cuddly toys, as well as an array of paints and other art materials (on the second top shelf, well out of reach).

*Right: A simple trellis rack hung from
the ceiling stores soft toys in this young
child's bedroom, and mobiles can be
hung from it too.*

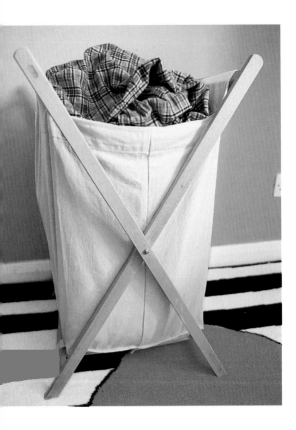

*A versatile laundry hamper made of
canvas hung on a folding wooden frame
can be collapsed flat and put away when
it is emptied on wash day. An accessible
upright container like this would also
be useful for storing dressing-up clothes
in a child's room.*

PLANNING FOR THE FUTURE

THE SOLUTION TO THE PROBLEM OF STORING a family in a home meant for one or
two people is probably to move. This is not an option open to everyone, of
course, but whether you move now or later, you need to make a plan to fulfill not only
your present storage requirements, but also your likely future ones. Now that you have
a family and are looking to the future, you will find that your priorities and your idea of
"useful" have undergone a change.

So, step one in tackling the problem is to reduce your own burden of possessions. Step
two is to plan realistically. When a baby arrives, however large it is, you will have difficulty
thinking of it as an enormous teenager, possibly taller than you, with as many (or nearly
as many) clothes, books, and other things as you have. The years until this happens will
pass more quickly than you thought possible, however. Of course, some items such as
large toys are held in common between children, and others are passed down according
to age. But the fact remains that if you have children, each one is another whole person
added to the household, a whole person rapidly accompanied by an amazing quantity of
his or her own belongings. Plan your storage space accordingly.

One method of calculating how much you will need is simple multiplication. Look at
the amount of space occupied by your and your partner's coats and boots by the back
door, for example, and more than double it if you plan to have two children. Triple it
(at least) for four, and add still more for baby carriers, diaper bags, and other bulky
equipment that awaits the family exodus from the house. Consider the way in which you
store, clean, and dry laundry, and multiply the space you will need for this. In the kitchen,
look at the space taken up for storing everyday plates and glasses. If you have just two

children, you will need double or more (allowing for little hangers-on) at every meal at which you all sit down together. This exercise is a tool to aid imagination, which in turn will help you plan with realism.

MANAGING POSSESSIONS

PLANNING IS NOT ENOUGH, however. One of the responsibilities of parenthood is that you have to become a manager of possessions, your own and your children's. This management involves continuous, or at the least regular, reassessment of each child's size, shape, reading age, interests, abilities, and sentiments with reference to clothes, shoes, toys, games, and books. You also have to be a diplomat, managing the transferral or disappearance of their possessions sensitively, so that their feelings are not hurt. No parent gets it right every time.

Another step in solving the problem of storing the family is acceptance, preferably by everyone in the household but at least by the adults, that possessions bring responsibility. Think about where you put something rather than simply plopping it down in the nearest place. Encourage children from an early age to understand that if they leave a toy on the floor it is more likely to be lost or broken than if it gets put in a toy box. Books, too, will get damaged if left lying around. Markers will dry out if left without tops, and will be lost unless returned to a pencil box. It really does pay to look after your stuff.

One of the keys to success in this area is accessibility. Accessible storage will be used, or is more likely to be used, than storage that is difficult or inconvenient. Convenient storage is well ordered, clearly labeled or color-coded and, especially where children are concerned, easy to reach. It is also close to the place where the objects are used. It may even be desirable to have more than one place for storing one type of thing – some dolls in the children's bedrooms, some in a playroom or play area in a living room.

CHILDREN IN THE KITCHEN

IN THE MODERN HOME, the hub of family activity is usually the kitchen, a room to which toys inevitably migrate. To stop yourself being driven mad by this, have a basket or box in which to keep stray toys in the kitchen before returning them to their proper

The space beneath this staircase has been cleverly used by creating cubbyholes and cupboards that continue the geometric pattern of the stairs' contemporary wooden balustrade. Large toys and crates of smaller toys fit in easily and are accessible. The cupboards are painted black – if this were blackboard paint, it would give even greater scope for children's activities.

A contemporary Shaker basket, designed to fit on the steps of a staircase and act as a collection point for all those little things that belong upstairs but are left lying around downstairs. When it is full (or when you are going up) you take it up and empty it.

place. This is not a toy box as such, merely a staging post or corral in which to contain the errant objects temporarily. They can then be taken en masse and distributed to their proper storage places. This makes tidying much easier than if you are trying to balance an armful of loose toys. Alternatively, have a toy box or cupboard in the kitchen, if there is sufficient space, but be prepared to have periodic sorting-out sessions when it threatens to overflow.

In general, adults have lost the natural creativity that prompts children to draw, paint and "make things" almost constantly and without a trace of self-consciousness or restraint. The kitchen is a sensible place to keep the equipment for these messy activities – aprons, plastic tablecloth, pens and pencils, tape, paints and brushes, old jam jars, scissors and glue, clay, and cutters.

To go with these, allow space for a number of separate and clearly labeled boxes containing paper of various types and colors, stickers, stencils, coloring books, old magazines, and holiday cards (for cutting pictures from), bits of cardboard, and all the other clutter that brings joy to the creative child. A generous box of scrap paper to which children have access is essential both for them and for you – so that they do not endlessly ask you for paper to draw on and so that you can easily write the lists that will help you be an organized, caring, and sane parent.

It is also sensible to keep a box or basket for books permanently in the kitchen, or set aside a section of accessible shelves for children's books, especially if the room is large enough for an armchair or sofa where an adult and child can snuggle up together for some reading. This book box, too, will probably need regular sorting and replenishment.

Children love to explore the contents of kitchen cupboards, so secure these with child safety locks. In order that your little angel does not feel totally excluded when you are busy making meals, you could leave one cupboard or deep drawer accessible – the one in which you store pan lids and baking sheets, perhaps, so that they can have fun emptying it all out without endangering themselves or the objects.

Teenagers are notorious for leaving homework books, magazines, and clothing around the house. One solution is to have a portable container such as a large wicker basket or canvas shopping bag into which you put their possessions that have "crept" in this way. At the end of each day, present the young person with this collection, saying, "These are yours. Put them away please." Alternatively, you may have to undertake a serious program of retraining.

Small children have an effect on storage in every room in the house. Nothing fragile, valuable, or dangerous should be stored where a child can reach it, and a small child can reach surprisingly high, especially if there is something to stand on or climb up. Remember

to make allowance for the fact that at the age of two the average child is half its adult height – 3 feet for a boy who will grow to 6 feet tall, a few inches less for a girl, for example – and his or her arm stretches some way beyond this. Console yourself with the thought that (with any luck) your child should grow out of the grab-it-and-destroy phase by the age of four, quite possibly earlier.

ADULT STORAGE NEEDS

IF YOUR HOUSE IS LARGE ENOUGH, you could designate one room, a dining room, living room, or study perhaps, as an adults-only area and store or display your fragile treasures here. Conversely, another room in the house could be soundproofed and designated the "den" for volume-addicted teenagers. While thinking about such things, consider in what ways your own possessions (and consequent storage requirements) are likely to increase over the coming years as opposed to your children's and your child-related ones. While children acquire toys and games, the sort of things adults accumulate are books, pictures, and objects, music recorded on CDs or other media, sports equipment, photographs, documents, financial records and other paperwork, computer and office equipment. If you collect a particular item, you are likely to need more storage/display space as your collection grows.

You will also acquire more clothes and footwear, balanced to some extent by discarding similar worn-out or unfashionable items. Pressure on storage space, however, may mean that it becomes worthwhile introducing a seasonal storage system for some of your clothes. As spring turns to summer, pack your heaviest winter woolens and coats into old suitcases suitably treated with moth repellent, or, if you have the space in your attic, in drawers and wardrobes there.

The advantage of an attic wardrobe is that your garments hang loose. The advantage of the suitcase method is that you can lug down the whole suitcase when you want the things in the autumn. When you bring them down, put away your flimsiest summer garments. All this may seem a chore. Instead, try to think of it as a celebrated ceremony, something to anticipate with pleasure, a signal that glorious summer is approaching, or hoary winter when you can look forward to hot, buttered toast by cozy, glowing fires.

Some adults in the family may have special needs – the elderly and the disabled, for instance. To make storage easy for them, it needs primarily to be physically accessible and, obviously, appropriate to their needs. Cupboard doors could have touch-release

A quiet cabin (above), with plenty of shelves for storing books, has been created in the space that is available because of the height of the ceiling. If you have small noisy children and sufficient space, a room that is exclusively for adults, where you can store, display, and enjoy your own books and treasures, is a sanctuary.

Antique toys are charming to look at but probably too fragile to be used by any but a very careful child. This charming little shelf unit, hung on the wall, offers space in which to display the old toys and enjoy their appearance (as well as the decorative spines of the books behind).

magnetic closers, for example, rather than being opened with a knob that you have to grip and turn. As with any other member of the household, consult them about what they want from storage before you start planning.

HEIRLOOMS

ANOTHER STORAGE SYSTEM that you need to devise in a family is the one for treasured heirlooms. Some clothes and toys are beautiful in themselves, well crafted from fine materials and far from worn out when your children have finished with them. You can pass them on to friends and relatives who have children, as you do with ordinary clothes and toys, or you can keep them safely for future generations to treasure. Most young parents would be delighted to be entrusted with things that were theirs when they were children – the quality is likely to surpass later standards, which usually decline rather than improve.

While doing this, you could also consider archiving some of your own clothes, the ones you cannot bear to part with but have not worn for several years. These can be stored, either for dressing up when the children are older, or until your children are old enough actually to wear them (or give them to a museum) because they are classics, perhaps made by a famous designer. You may even surprise yourself and wish to wear them again one day. Pack them carefully, ideally with acid-free tissue paper (not forgetting moth repellent), and clearly label the boxes or suitcases in which you archive them, or indeed any item.

THE GROWING CHILD

AS CHILDREN GROW UP, their bedrooms change. Well-planned storage can grow and change with them. A baby's room needs storage for bulky items like diapers, linens, cotton, baby wipes, lotions, and so on, together with somewhere to change the diaper and a nonporous trash can. Soft toys need a shelf or box to get them up off the floor. Even at this stage, girls need different storage for clothes from boys because they have dresses that should be hung from a rail, preferably inside a wardrobe for protection. Until they have suits or jackets, boys do not actually need hanging space, as their trousers, shirts, sweaters, and so on can lie flat in drawers.

The ideal teenager's room (left) looks grown-up, but still has space on a top shelf for those beloved old childhood toys. It has a desk for schoolwork, plenty of bookshelves, space for a music system and compact discs, and above all, a funky appearance.

A low cupboard with a broad top where you can change the baby, storing the diapers beneath, can later be transformed into storage for clothes, toys, or bedding. The top can then be used to store a dollhouse, fort, or other large, handsome toy. A sturdy chest of drawers will see a child through to young adulthood and beyond, as will a simple, tall wardrobe. Shelves built into this to accommodate many layers of small garments and objects can be removed as the child grows in stature.

It is easier to keep track of children's shoes if they are not on the floor. Instead, store them on the bottom of a wardrobe, in a basket, or in a cart of the type with shallow shelves designed primarily for kitchens. A small cart like this can be wheeled into a tight corner or under a sink and wheeled out again for the once-daily choice of shoes.

A tall bookcase, or an area of enclosed shelves climbing up the wall, is one of the most useful storage items in a child's bedroom, especially in a small room. It provides versatile storage from babyhood to adulthood, fulfilling the child's needs and desires throughout that time. The distance between the shelves needs to be variable in order to accommodate the different sizes of books and other possessions as the child grows up. Inexpensive mass-produced softwood bookcases can be customized simply by drilling extra peg holes at intervals down the side supports. Softwood can also be painted, to make the bookcases hard wearing, and repainted in accordance with the child's changing taste in interior decoration.

TOYS AND BOOKS

WHEN THE CHILD IS SMALL, the top shelves, out of his or her reach, are ideal for heirlooms or other fragile toys, as well as the inevitable articles that the child considers vital to happiness but in fact never or rarely plays with. Here, they are on

These shelves (above), used for storing toys, games, and books, are attached to the wall; adjustable shelving gives you more flexibility as the child turns into a teenager.

Opposite: There is space for a poster of a pop group in front of a teenager's desk, which has plenty of room for the computer.

Below: A vertical storage system for computer disks. You slide one into each separate pocket – because it is clear plastic, you can see the labels at a glance.

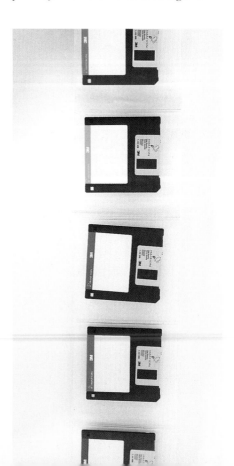

view, which reassures the child, but safe, which satisfies the adult. If children of different ages are sharing a room, the older child can store treasures here out of reach of the younger one.

Next, at adult shoulder height, is the place for boxes of jigsaw puzzles and board games stacked on top of each other. If these are tipped out and muddled, a huge amount of work is the result (for the adult, mainly), so it is worth keeping them just out of reach of the child, but easily accessible for an adult to produce one at a time.

Below this comes a shelf, or part of a shelf, devoted to dressing-table possessions such as hairbrushes and combs, hair bands and ties (for a girl), a china piggy bank, and a photograph of a favorite aunt/friend/godmother. Next come books, which are better stored in short spans than large; otherwise, they all fall over untidily. If necessary, consider installing dividers to create smaller sections of shelf for books, rather like cubbyholes, or use heavy bookends to maintain order. Upright books are easier to take off the shelf to read, and easier to put away too.

The bottom shelf or two house open-top plastic crates of toys. The plastic box in its many forms and colors is an item that the modern parent worships. It is light, transportable, accessible, jolly to look at, washable – its fine qualities seem endless. Two of these stacked on the bottom shelf of a bookcase provide enough capacity for all a child's loose toys. The child can see in (don't have the shelf above too low) and reach in for individual toys, or pull the whole box onto the floor to explore the contents. On the shelf above, or stacked elsewhere in the room or in the playroom, you can have similar boxes (they are obtainable in many shapes, sizes, and colors), each containing a separate set of toys.

A set of toys is a collection of pieces that work together to make an environment or that allow children to enact a situation, which fulfills quite complex play needs and enables them to develop skills – creative, social, or motor – as well as giving them hours of fun. Examples of important toy sets are a fort and soldiers; building blocks; a farm with outbuildings, animals, people, and tractors; a Noah's ark or zoo; Lego blocks, tools, and an engine; a cassette player and tapes; a baby doll with clothes, bedding, bottle, bath; a model-girl doll with clothes, bike, car, boat, or horse; a china tea service complete with teapot and lid; a stove, pans, and play food; a train set; plastic model people in a hospital ward, garage, or police station; a dollhouse.

A well-equipped child's room or playroom has at least one of these, often more, and they are played with, and give pleasure, over a considerable number of years. It is important to keep a set together, separate from others, and labeled. A child is not attracted to play with toys that are dirty or broken. If there is room, a small desk or work

table for quiet writing/drawing/homework is another item that a child will find useful for many years from a surprisingly early age.

Other practical and lightweight forms of toy storage are provided by such things as the pocketed toy organizer, a tall, narrow fabric or plastic panel with large pockets at intervals down the front; and the toy hammock, useful in the bathroom (for wet toys) as well as the bedroom (for soft toys). Neither of these is really suitable for heavy toys. The hammock is related to another item invaluable to the parent of young children, the net bag (see page 57).

THE TEENAGER

TEENAGERS have different storage requirements for their bedrooms. The toys have mostly gone, although a hard-core of seemingly babyish ones with special sentimental value remains. The bookcase remains vital, now mainly for books. A desk or work table is now a necessity, possibly with space for a computer. You may find it necessary to invest in a proper computer table with a pull-out shelf for the keyboard and a shelf below that for a printer. The room is likely to have a music system accompanied with a quantity of recordings, and a frame bed is likely to be bargained away in favor of a platform or sofa bed that can double as seating for the child and friends. A chest bed with drawers beneath has the advantage of offering down storage.

Clothes are, of course, larger and there are probably more of them, especially for a girl, who may want a large mirror, either over a sink or full-length. Sinks in bedrooms become especially useful as a house full of children becomes a house full of young adults, but sinks may take up room needed for other storage and furniture.

IDEA BOX

HAPPY FAMILIES

* Plan realistically for the future.
* Regularly sort your and your children's possessions.
* Seasonal storage will give you more space.
* Accessible, well-thought-out storage will help educate your children to be tidy.
* Try to make storage fun for children, too – for example, you can buy sturdy cardboard boxes printed with popular children's story or cartoon characters.
* Use plastic boxes, baskets, and net bags.
* Bookshelves can store many things besides books.
* Keep a few toys and books in the kitchen.
* Store paints and equipment for messy play in the kitchen.
* Allow children access to the kitchen cupboard where you store unbreakables like pie pans.
* Assess their storage needs as your offspring grow from babies to "big" children.
* Teenagers want a bedroom/ sitting room with storage for computer/music/clothes.
* Take one family room with a fireplace. Raise the opening for the fire 18 inches off the floor (with a hearth correspondingly high). Build cupboards under the hearth and continue them both ways to the edge of the room. Result: loads of floor-level storage for toys.

CHAPTER ELEVEN

SMALL URBAN SPACES

This astonishing apartment (left) in an old school library has a wall of cupboards, built to house television and music systems but also to disguise the fact that the owner had no other possessions. Each alcove has its own lighting.

The bedroom looks down over the sitting room. "Leaving it open like this made the bedroom seem large," says the architect, Robert Wilson. It opens directly from the stairs, which are supported by a molded aluminum "spine."

LIVING IN A CITY generally means living in a small space. It doesn't necessarily mean having to live in cramped quarters, however. There are many techniques for making the most of a small apartment or house. Keeping the place in perfect order is one. Every inch of space has to earn its living, which generally means having storage built in rather than freestanding.

Throughout a small home, remember that shallow storage is as useful, if not as spacious, as deep storage. Shallow shelves and cupboards can hold books, china, glass, and all your other belongings just as well, so look for sites for such storage. If there isn't sufficient room for cupboard doors to swing open, or if they would be inconvenient, have sliding doors, folding accordian doors made from wood or MDF panels, or a blind instead.

Face cupboard fronts and line the wall behind shelves with mirrors to create an illusion of depth, except in the kitchen where a mirror can quickly become steamy and greasy. Here you can use sheet stainless steel, which has a reflective sheen and is easy to keep clean. If you line the wall of an alcove with a mirror to the edge, this will give the impression of there being a room beyond. Hang a picture over the mirror, or place a piece of furniture in front of it, if there is any danger of someone walking into it.

Boats, especially broad-beam barges, are an appealing source of inspiration for squeezing as much storage as possible into a small space. If you can visit such a boat, notice how little doors fold down in corners and under steps to provide storage space behind. Furniture is built in, and every seat has drawers beneath or a hinged seat that lifts to reveal a void. No space is wasted.

Sliding doors are no longer considered poor relations of ones that swing or fold open. They have thrown off their flimsy 1970s image and become an invaluable tool for architects grappling with the problem of making a small home feel spacious. This one is a huge orange slab set invisibly into runners in the floor and ceiling. Closed, it looks like part of the wall; open, it reveals the main bedroom beyond. The bedroom has plenty of storage in tall wardrobes, and also storage in the base of the bed.

A bathroom sink, set at a right angle to the exterior wall rather than flat against it, creates a dressing area beyond, equipped with tall built-in wardrobes.

A clever solution to the problem of where to put the kitchen in a small house. This room is mainly a sitting room (above), but one end (at the back of the house, tucked in beside the stairs) is the kitchen (right). This is hidden by a wall that does not reach the ceiling, thereby allowing the eye to move beyond it, creating an illusion of extra space. This also means that the person cooking in the tiny galley is not excluded from conversation.

The late David Hicks made brilliant use of limited space in his London apartment. The kitchen is cleverly concealed in two built-in cupboards, one on each side of the desk in his hall. The right-hand one contains a sink, stove and storage; the left-hand cupboard (out of sight) hides the fridge. Witty, well-thought-out details include a door on the front of the plinth of the sculpture to the right, which opens to reveal the trash can. Other plinths conceal a broom cupboard and more storage. The magnificent desk itself acts as a visual focus for the room when the cupboards are closed and has pull-out shelves at each side to store drinks and an ice bucket.

The photographs on this page show the clever use of one room in a town apartment. The top picture shows how the main room is split into two areas: kitchen and dining. The galley kitchen has been designed as a raised platform behind an impressive stainless-steel block of units. Not an inch of space is wasted: The stairs to the kitchen store drawers in the risers (see below), and the space below the kitchen units is full of cupboards that store essential household items (bottom).

Stair-riser storage (above). Free-wheeling drying rack and trash can (below).

THE KITCHEN AND LIVING AREAS

IN A SMALL HOME, it is even more vital than in a large one to set priorities for the use of your general living areas. The first question is: "How important is the kitchen?" Is it used only occasionally, because you are single or childless, eat out frequently, and rarely entertain? Or is it a family room, the focus of the household's social life, a place for regular cooking and eating?

If your kitchen is rarely used, it need hardly be more than cupboard-sized. In fact, it could be in a cupboard whose doors or shutters, when closed across the front, conceal it completely. A kitchen concealed in this way can be quite extensive, stretching along the wall and giving you plenty of storage space, but it is nonetheless invisible when the doors are closed.

Alternatively, you can conceal a small cooking area in one corner of your living room behind a folding screen or angled sliding or folding doors. Or you can tuck it behind a "floating" wall constructed across one end of the room. This is a solid wall that finishes short of the ceiling and walls of the room, creating a screen to which the kitchen, work surface and equipment can be attached. When working in the kitchen, you can hear and talk to other people, but they cannot see you or the clutter of culinary creation. A similar screen that stops at shoulder height would give you some above-counter storage on a shallow shelf, while not excluding you from the rest of the room's activities.

If the kitchen is the household's main living room, you could dispense with the concept of a separate sitting room and create a living kitchen with a small sofa and as big a table as there is space for. This makes sense if you have children, as they usually gravitate to the kitchen and play there, even in a large house and even if there is another room officially designated as a playroom.

To increase the sense of space in a small kitchen, replace the center part of the cupboard doors with a screen of chicken wire or other mesh, or glass, transparent or translucent. Doors that open take up space and can become a nuisance, so you could remove them altogether, having open shelves. Instead of wall cupboards above the counter, which make a room seem smaller by creating a solid block at eye level, keep the back wall in view and use open shelves, hooks, and racks for storage. Square storage jars or canisters use limited space more efficiently than round ones. Have the microwave on a shelf, not taking up space on the counter.

In a very small space, you can create a narrower-than-usual counter simply by slicing a strip off the back edge, and the same principle can be applied to units. In a kitchen that is rectangular but too narrow for two rows of units opposite each other, you can either build the counter deeper than standard or have bookshelves along the wall opposite the units. Bookshelves don't have to be used for books – they are ideal for storing pans, jars, cans, and bottles. Deeper-than-usual units give you added storage space, but the backs of shelves or cupboards can become muddled. Use plastic boxes or baskets to organize the inner recesses, gathering like with like and making things at the back more easily accessible.

Inside cupboards, if you have them, use can be squeezed out of every storage space with plastic-coated wire organizers of the type available in good hardware stores. These include baskets that hang from the shelf above, racks for hanging wineglasses, and, simplest of all, the ladder stand. This is a sturdy, rectangular wire stand with legs, which you place over a pile of plates. This instantly creates another layer of storage on which to put more china, or whatever the cupboard contains.

In a small city home, there often is not space for the whole range of full-sized machinery such as a dishwasher, oven, refrigerator-freezer, and microwave that you might expect to find in a large family kitchen. If the kitchen is used only for breakfast and snacks, you don't, in any case, need them. It is not necessary to do without completely, however. Designers and manufacturers have developed an increasingly impressive range of slimline and combination models for the small kitchen that, unfortunately, are not correspondingly small in price.

There is the microwave that also combines the functions of a grill and a small conventional oven; the mini dishwasher that pulls out like a drawer; the all-in-one kitchen that has a small sink alongside two stove-top burners, with a combination microwave beneath and a refrigerator under that, all fitted into the size of a standard unit; and, perhaps most ingenious of all, the two-burner unit that sits on your work surface when wanted and flips up against the back wall when not in use to give you more space for food preparation. Any of these will leave you more space for storage in a tiny kitchen.

This music-lover (and accomplished pianist) has a large collection of CDs, which can be seen in the background here, on shelves that are exactly the right size. Having built-in shelves designed to accommodate one type or size of object is usually the most space-efficient form of storage, vital in a small urban space.

A Japanese-style interior has bedroom wardrobes with tall sliding doors. Inside, there are shelves for clothes and hats, a tie rack, and an appealing chest of small drawers, stepped like a staircase.

If you have room for a conventional sink, consider installing one that has no drainer attached to the side. Instead, fix a plate rack or drying rack above the bowl of the sink itself, into which water can drip. Alternatively, have a folding draining rack on a plastic tray alongside the sink. When the rack is not in use, you can fold it flat and store it and the tray while using the surface for other activities.

In the sitting area, simply follow the principles of down storage and up storage to maximize the floor space. Up storage becomes especially important in a small home. Look for places in every room where you can build shelves above head height, perhaps running all round the room above doors and windows. Back at floor level, furniture made of plastic and other lightweight materials takes on a new importance, as do folding and stacking chairs and tables – have out only the minimum seating you need for daily use and store the rest away for visitors.

BEDROOMS

IN AN URBAN HOME where space is at a premium, storage under the bed, and even behind a hinged headboard, becomes even more valuable. A bed that is low on the floor, such as a futon on a frame, is not as effective as a high-level bed with plenty of boxes, drawers, or cupboards underneath. The cupboards do not have to have doors, which need space into which to swing open, but can simply be cubbyholes for storing books, clothes, and shoes.

A studio apartment requires special cunning in making the most of minimal space. Here, with sufficient height, you could "store" the sleeping area on top of a tiny kitchen and bathroom, leaving the main room as a living area. In any arrangement where the bedroom is raised up, or in a gallery, have open-tread, ladder-type access to the upper level, rather than a solid staircase, which will create a visual barrier.

The type of bed that folds up against the wall is another space-saving alternative for the urban home. (See Chapter Eight, page 80, for more about wall beds.) Build storage shelves on the wall above the folded-up bed and hang a blind or curtain that, when extended, will hide the entire wall. Bunk beds that fold away are useful in a children's room, but you lose the advantage of the copious storage space that can be built in underneath a high-level bed that is a permanent structure.

Clothes storage becomes a greater issue in a confined space. Part of the solution is, unfortunately for those to whom it does not come naturally, to be disciplined and ruthless about how many clothes you have. Seasonal storage, where you put away winter clothes in summer and summer clothes in winter, will help the situation if you have an attic or

A mirror is a useful tool for creating an illusion of space. In this bedroom (left) it acts as a headboard on the wall that screens the dressing room, at the same time reflecting the handsome sash windows.

other place in which to stash away a couple of old suitcases. Otherwise, the same strictures that apply to organizing your clothes in a more generous space apply here, only more so.

If you are naturally a very tidy person, consider banishing your wardrobe doors, which shrink the room by creating a visual barrier. Alternatively, remove doors that swing open conventionally and use instead sliding panels, folding doors, or a curtain that hangs flat or almost flat when drawn closed. As in living spaces, maximum use of up storage is vital, and fitted furniture, built into the available space, is more efficient than freestanding. If your wardrobe finishes short of the ceiling, consider extending it upwards to create not-used-often storage space.

Where there is space for a shallow cupboard, but not a wardrobe deep enough to accommodate hanging clothes, consider installing a pull-out cupboard of the type that also makes use of space under staircases (see Chapter Thirteen, page 150). This cupboard would be wide enough for coat hangers, which you hook over a rod attached to the door of the cupboard, set at a right angle to the wall rather than parallel to it as in a conventional wardrobe.

THE BATHROOM

WITH THE RANGE OF SLIM CABINETS that is available today it is possible to fit a bathroom quite easily into a small space. At the same time, you don't want your tiny bathroom to feel claustrophobic or cluttered. A bathroom, however small, should be relaxing, a pleasure to spend time in, and it needs sufficient storage space to hide all the bottles of lotions and potions, not to mention first-aid items and pills, that are generally kept here.

Efficient extraction is vital in a bathroom, as it is in any kitchen, but especially so in a small one. It will enable you to use plenty of mirrors (make sure that these are toughened

Mirrors attached to the wardrobe doors in this passageway make it seem much larger than it is, and also introduce warm, rich color by reflecting the decorations of the room beyond.

*Opposite: Another solution to
bathroom storage.*

or laminated to help avoid injury if they should shatter), particularly on the front of large, shallow cupboards at eye level. Or you could commission a mural painter to decorate your cupboards. If a professionally painted mural is beyond your means, you could face the cupboards with an enlarged reproduction of a painting, well varnished for protection.

Glass shelves fixed across a window provide extra surface area, but select your bottles and jars for storage here with care as they will be highly visible. If necessary, transfer your bubble bath and shampoo into more handsome bottles. Another surface that can be converted to storage is the back of the bathroom door, to which you can attach long, narrow boxes with high sides that will hold your supplies safely when the door is swung open.

Installing a shower rather than a bath is an obvious space-saver, but if you are passionate about soaking in the tub, there are compact, deep baths that might provide a solution, and even a hip bath, in which you sit rather than lie. A shower door made of suitable glass takes up less room and gives more space in the shower than a curtain. Inside the shower, have a fixed or hanging rack for soap, shampoo, and sponge.

*The bathroom of this interior, designed
by Charles Rutherfoord, has a wall
of cupboards whose doors are faced with
mirrors. Behind each door are rows of
drawers. You can see exactly what is in
each, because they have clear fronts. The
mirrors make the bathroom look huge;
behind the tiled screen that follows the
curve of the bath is a toilet on one side
and shower on the other.*

In a bathroom with room for a full-sized bathtub, check that you are using the space around and beneath the body of the bath efficiently. If it is boxed in, is there a cupboard in the boxing for hiding ugly items like cleaning materials? If it is not boxed in, use the space beneath the tub for storage, with the aid of flat baskets or a shallow box on castors. If you are installing a bath, have it built in at a level that is higher than normal, with drawers or small cupboards built into the space beneath. Or, use this extra space to install a space-saving room heater of the type designed for use in a damp environment like a bathroom.

To relieve pressure on the bathroom, consider installing small hand sinks in the bedrooms, especially children's bedrooms, so that washing up and bedtime activities like tooth-brushing do not necessarily monopolize the bathroom. This may be a particularly wise precaution as you approach your children's teenage years. Likewise, you might consider having the toilet in a separate tiny room rather than in the bathroom, so that they can be used separately, in privacy, at the same time by different people.

The bathroom, or the kitchen if there is sufficient space, is a possible location for a utility "room," more accurately a cupboard that as nearly as possible serves the function of a utility room. If you have a separate clothes dryer and washer, stack these securely on top of each other and have shelves above for household goods. Once again, sliding or folding doors will take up less room than swinging ones.

OUT OF DOORS

IF YOU HAVE A SMALL OUTDOOR AREA or garden that nonetheless needs maintenance, store tools in a cupboard of the type made of galvanized metal and designed to bolt directly to an external wall. These come in various sizes. A cupboard of this sort could also be used to hide unsightly trash cans and protect them from marauding dogs and urban wildlife. If there is no room to store a bicycle, it could be hung on a large peg or pin on an outside wall, secured to it with a padlock.

* Take inspiration from clever storage on board boats.
* Build shallow storage cupboards in narrow spaces.
* Use mirrors on front of cupboards and at the back of shelves (stainless steel in kitchen) to create an illusion of space.
* Install slimline or combination models of kitchen appliances.
* Or, have a family kitchen as your whole living room.
* Store pans and jars on a bookshelf in the kitchen.
* Use racks and stands to make the most of every square inch inside cupboards.
* In a high-ceilinged studio apartment, "store" the sleeping area on top of kitchen and bathroom.
* Have a sofabed, wall bed, chest bed, or built-in bed with storage beneath.
* Restrain and organize your possessions, and your wardrobe.
* Install a shower or small deep bath.
* Glass shelves across windows offer extra storage surfaces.
* In a narrow or wedge-shaped bedroom, have a wall-to-wall bed constructed by a cabinetmaker, with cupboards at the accessible end and more storage in the base, then have a mattress specially made to fit the size and shape of the bed.

CHAPTER TWELVE

SECRET SPACES

Opposite: A dressing room has been created in the passage leading from the landing to the bathroom. Hidden behind the silk curtains is generous wardrobe space. Curtains are ideal here, because there is no room for doors to swing open.

You have to look twice to see the doors in this wall; the chair rail, dado, and wall color continue across them, and pictures are hung on them to help them "disappear." The picture hung above, across both, also confuses the eye.

ONE OF THE EXCITEMENTS of making a systematic survey of your home in preparation for transforming your storage is finding space that you had forgotten was there. Usually, this space is filled with things that were put there either "temporarily" several years ago, or because there was an empty space and you were looking for somewhere to dump things that have no proper home. Attics, basements, and garages are prime places for such "lost" or forgotten surprise spaces.

The first thing to do with these spaces is to empty them and distribute the objects along the lines described in Chapter Two (page 22). Throw and give away as much as possible. Then clean the space thoroughly and try to look at it as if you had never seen it before, considering how it could be used creatively.

Is it a tall, narrow space where, if you installed a rail, you could hang out-of-season or vintage clothes in bags or a hanging "wardrobe"? Is it a square space that would neatly accommodate crates or boxes? Is it an oddly shaped space that would become useful if you installed shelves? Is it a space that is easy to get at on a daily basis and could be useful as a site for a recycling system, for example? Or is it inaccessible and useful only for long-term storage? Is it dry? Is it damp? Is it warm?

An inaccessible warm, damp place has probably got things growing in it and needs professional attention, but almost every other type of space can be used for storage of some sort. The same principles apply as to any other part of the home: Store like with like; get things off the floor with racks, hooks, shelves; use transparent containers or label everything clearly.

Below, a home office is hidden in a floor-to-ceiling cupboard with generous deep shelves for all the necessary records. Paperwork and clutter are tidied away in ring binders and box files within the cupboard. The sofa folds out into a spare bed, so that the room serves a dual purpose.

When the door is closed (above left) it is invisible, because of the plaster cast attached to the front of it, which is part of this hall's dramatic styling and decoration. When it is open (above) you realize that you have succumbed to a delicious trick. Anything hung on the front of a door needs to be secured with care in order not to risk it flying off when the door is flung open.

Architect Jason Cooper made a leap of
imagination when asked to create space
in this small apartment. He removed the
bathroom. Instead, sink and toilet are concealed in a cupboard. The bath (left)
is under the bed, sunk into a raised floor.
The bed moves aside on grooves in the
floor, and there are trapdoors elsewhere
in the floor that lift to reveal quantities of
storage. The apartment is open plan, with
shelves built into every possible wall, but
the bedroom can be concealed for privacy
simply by dropping bamboo blinds (left
below and below).

Do not throw away old kitchen cabinets – re-site them in the basement, garage, or tool shed where they can continue to be useful, storing tools and nails, things used rarely, or as here, garden equipment.

THE BASEMENT

BASEMENTS VARY HUGELY, from a tiny room in which you can barely stand upright to vast caverns. If your basement is very damp, you could have it lined with plastic or waterproof paint to make it dry. A slightly damp basement can be made use of. Traditional whitewash will keep the walls clean. Build your shelves on materials that won't rot, like stone or concrete, and use duckboards to walk on. These can be propped up on the stairs to dry during the winter months. Be sensible about what you store in a damp basement, and keep things in plastic rather than in cardboard boxes.

Some basements are raised slightly above ground level so that they have windows, ventilation, and daylight, albeit rather high up the wall. Where the house is on a slope, the basement floor can be at or near ground level on one side of the house. This type of basement obviously gives you the greatest scope for conversion to a useful storage space.

Many people have their utility room in the basement. If the central-heating furnace is there too, the room may be warm and sufficiently dry to hang up wet laundry – an extractor fan will quickly help to adjust the humidity – as well as to store cleaning materials and other household items. And basement rooms are useful as playrooms, with space for large things such as a Ping-Pong table or train set.

The very first steps to take to convert an under-used basement into a place of which you can be proud are to paint it white or a fresh, light color, and to install bright light. Bare brick, stone, or concrete block should be sealed with an appropriate primer and whitewashed or covered with an exterior paint. Light fittings can be utilitarian, but if the ceiling is low choose types where the bulb is protected by a wire cage or plastic cover. If you intend to use this area for laundry or a hobby that involves electrical equipment, have several extra electrical sockets installed in appropriate places. These will probably be more accessible placed a yard or so up the wall rather than at ground level.

For shelving, choose an inexpensive mass-produced system of the type where you can design your own combination of shelves, racks, cupboards, and so on. You simply buy the component parts and assemble them in your own configuration. Remember that if the system is made of timber you can easily customize it with added rails and hooks and by drilling extra holes for different shelf heights.

Assuming it is dry and relatively cool, the basement can be a useful adjunct to the kitchen, for storing food, wine, and equipment. Have a flat surface available – ideally cool slate or stone, though ordinary shelves will do – so that when you are preparing food for a party or celebration, finished dishes can be brought here to await the occasion. If you make a batch of marmalade or chutney, store the jars here until you are ready to

This basement is made to work in several different ways at once. It is a laundry room, workshop, shower room, and sometime playroom. It is painted white and equipped with plenty of artificial light.

The white paint and light fittings compensate for there being only one small window (most basements do not even have this); it has been transformed from a dark, underground dungeon.

distribute them or eat the contents. Canned food, oils and vinegars, preserves, and anything in a sealed container can be kept in a cellar.

The basement is the ideal place to store china, glass, and equipment that are not used often but are invaluable at the right time. Large platters, a fish kettle and special fish-shaped dishes, a smoker or crock pot that is rarely used, holiday china, extra glasses for parties – such things are used infrequently but regularly.

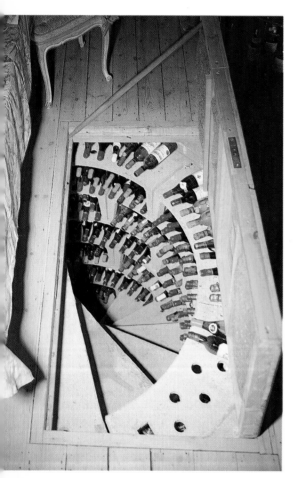

An ingeniously designed wine cellar of the type that can be sunk into the ground under the floor of a home that does not have a conventional basement – it goes no farther than you can see here. You walk down the concrete spiral steps; bottles are stored on curved shelves on the wall of the cellar; holes in the shelves aid ventilation.

THE WINE CELLAR

WINE IS A SUBJECT on which enthusiasts can wax at length. Racks come in all sizes, from very small to wall sized, in a variety of materials. Some shelving systems have a bottle shelf, with ridges to support each bottle individually, among their options. You can make your own cellar system by stacking short lengths of terra-cotta or concrete pipes of appropriate diameter, securing them with blobs of cement.

Ideally, bottles should be laid on their sides so that the cork remains damp and no air can reach the wine, and so that any sediment settles on the bottom. The air should not be liable to fluctuations in temperature, 60°F being the ideal. The exact temperature is not so important if you are not going to keep the wine long. You can store white wines and rosés in an old refrigerator ready for instant consumption, but beware of keeping them too cold as this could detract from the flavor. Label each bottle around the neck so that you don't have to take it out to find out what it is.

An interesting way to store wine if your house or garden apartment does not have a basement is to construct one in the ground beneath your floor. A hole about 6 feet deep and square is dug and a prefabricated concrete structure built into it. This looks like a spiral staircase, around the outside edge of which are curved shelves for the bottles. You access the wine by walking down the steps. The roof of the cellar is a trapdoor in the floor above. Before ordering this compact wine cellar, consult a professional to be sure that it will not weaken the structure of the building.

THE ATTIC

THE SAME CLEAN-AND-LIGHT-IT approach recommended for the basement also applies to converting "lost" space in an attic or loft. After this, the problems here are likely to be different from those at the other extremity of the house. There, damp is usually a key concern. Here, sloping walls or roof is to be contended with. Clearly, the attic is not a place for expanses of shelving.

The first element to examine is the floor. It is possible to use an unfloored attic for storage, but only to a limited extent. Boxes and suitcases that will balance on the joists can be kept here, but even then there is a danger that they may crash through a ceiling below. Added to this, an unfloored attic that is insulated with fiberglass fluff may pose a health hazard, or at the least be an unpleasant place. If your attic is unfloored, consider getting a quotation from a carpenter to have it boarded over. Calculate how much storage space you would gain.

Left: Good use has been made here of attic space on each side of a chimney breast. Shelves (the same height on each side) offer storage for treasures and books, while cupboards below have doors that flip down, hinged at the bottom. Low bookshelves continue along the sides of the attic.

If there is already a floor, is it safe? If you are in doubt, have it surveyed and repaired. Is access satisfactory? If this is via a hatch and ladder, consider updating the latter to a type that opens down easily and offers a handrail. Some architects seem to believe that only very small people and objects will ever want to get into an attic, so remember that enlarging the hatch itself, in order to improve access, is usually a feasible option.

The narrowing space under the eaves can be utilized in various ways. The most sophisticated is to have storage bins made with angled backs that fit the slope of the roof. Equipped with castors and a handle at the front, the box can be pulled out for access. These "drawers" look smart and are ideal if your attic is also an occasional workroom, playroom, or sleeping space for visitors.

A simpler way of using the space under the eaves is to build a shelf along the length of the attic with room above and below it for two rows of well-labeled boxes. In front of these, place storage that can easily be moved for access to the boxes behind, such as hanging bags of garments that can be held aside like curtains, or clothes on a wheeled rack, or larger boxes on castors.

The attic is a useful place for furniture that is too worn for general exposure but still serviceable – here it can earn its keep by acting as a container for smaller items and clothes. If necessary, fix castors on the bottom so that it can easily be moved to gain access to things behind.

UNDER THE STAIRS AND ELSEWHERE

ONLY IF YOU LIVE IN A BUNGALOW, ranch house, or apartment is your home without under-stair space. Even apartments often have space under the stairs to upper floors. A tall town house can have several under-stair spaces, each of them with potential

This secret space makes marvelous use of a narrow slice of the bedroom, along the wall near the door. It houses wardrobes, cupboards that extend under the eaves on the right, bookshelves in the doorway, and above, plenty of storage space for boxes, baskets, and suitcases.

Wall space in this stairwell (right) has been cleverly used to display a collection of objects. These get plenty of natural light, and the owner can enjoy them every time she walks past.

Below: Part of this spacious landing has been commandeered as a working area, by tucking a table into the corner. This is an ideal arrangement; the person work-ing can enjoy the generous natural light and the handsome bookshelves and their contents, enhanced by the wall behind having been painted terra-cotta.

for storage. Unlike attic and basement, however, this storage space is a highly visible part of the main living area. You see it every time you walk past to go up or down the stairs. It must therefore be smart, discreet, and in keeping with the rest of the decorations.

Structures for built-in or specially constructed storage under stairs include cupboards, shelves, and pull-out racks. Think about which items you want to store here before deciding on any one option, and remember that they can be combined: cupboards below, display shelves above, for example. The potential disadvantage of shelves is that they will not make full use of the depth of the staircase, unless they are very deep, which is generally impractical. The advantage of shallow shelves is an increase in the feeling of space if the hallway alongside the stairs is narrow.

The simplest form of bulk storage under the stairs is a cupboard or cupboards. It is better to have doors along the side of the space rather than at the end. If access to the space has to be through a door at the end, devise a system of wheeled bins or carts that will allow you to get to items at the very back, even if only occasionally, and if possible do not store heavy items in this cupboard as they will act as a disincentive to access.

The space under stairs is so often wasted, or not used as well as it could be. Built-in furniture can make the most of awkward spaces. Here it provides a work space, with plenty of storage both below the desktop and above, in the cupboard built to look like a dresser.

Pull-out racks or cupboards are the most expensive option (unless you make them yourself), but they make excellent use of what can otherwise be dead space. Each rack can be double-sided, giving you a huge quantity of storage for small items appropriate to the room or area of the house, such as books, packages of food, files or boxes containing work or household records, or music on CD, tape, or vinyl. Racks such as these would also make good use of space under the stairs in a cellar.

Wherever they are sited in the house, the contents of the racks should not be items to which you need access very frequently – these should be in the appropriate room – unless the space is open plan. Another important point to remember when planning is that if the stairs are in a hallway or passage, the racks can pull out only as far as the width of the passage allows.

Old houses to which extra rooms have been added over the decades or centuries are the most likely to have strange corners and alcoves. Like the space under the stairs, these can be boxed in as cupboards or given shelves – in either case they will be transformed into useful storage.

T H E   G A R A G E

A GARAGE, if you have one, usually has room for storing some items in addition to the car. Use racks, hooks, and shelves on the walls for bicycles, outdoor furniture, and games. The space below the beams and above the hood of the car can be used by suspending a hanging shelf or shelves from the joists above or by hanging things such as folding garden furniture directly from hooks screwed into the beams. If there is room in one corner, an old refrigerator-freezer is useful for storing extra frozen food and as additional space for keeping dishes for a party or special occasion when you have prepared more food than will fit in your everyday refrigerator.

WORK SPACES

This tiny office (left) has been created in an alcove, in one corner of a drawing room, by cutting away the front of the desk in a curve. Cupboards below store ugly utilitarian files; shelves above store part of a large collection of books.

By storing some of your collection of postcards, garnered from exhibitions and galleries over many years, in a plastic container like this one, you can enjoy the front card and, of course, swap it for another whenever you feel like a change.

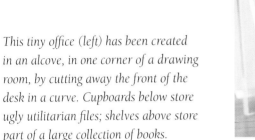

DEALISTS MAY HAVE A VISION of home as the place to which you go after a day's work, in order to relax and be enveloped by family warmth and nurturing. But to many people this is a paternalistic view, outdated and outmoded. The day's labor, whether paid employment or household management, is as likely to take place at home as anywhere outside at the dawn of the twenty-first century. Home may indeed be an oasis of relaxation, at certain times of the day or the week, but a great deal of hard work occurs there nonetheless.

The office shown in these three photographs (right, left, and below left) can disappear into the tower of cupboards in the corner. Tables and shelves slide out; when the large cupboard door is opened, the computer swings out on an arm. There is even a chest of drawers that draws out from one side of the tower. This is the ultimate hideaway office, but gadgets like the bracket arm, and simple ideas like having storage on castors, can make a reality of a similar, if less ambitious, disappearing office.

Magazine storage boxes come in a bewildering but thrilling range of colors, finishes, and materials. You can easily and cheaply customize your own, perhaps color coding different publications, by painting cardboard boxes.

A cupboard in one corner of this bathroom houses the washing machine, above, and wire mesh drawers for storing linen below. This is a clever arrangement if you do not have space for a separate utility room, but the washing machine must be well supported.

THE UTILITY ROOM

ANY HOME, especially a family home, runs smoothly and supplies the physical needs of its occupants only if at least one person in the household is a manager, organizing and stocking it, providing meals and clean laundry, ensuring a reasonable level of cleanliness, maintaining its safety and usefulness, and making it an attractive place to be. All these activities require equipment and materials, and storage.

The kitchen is the obvious powerhouse of a home, but there are other places that qualify as work spaces, where household business takes place. The first of these is the utility room. Almost all new houses are built with a utility room for laundry activities and for storing household and cleaning supplies, and many old homes too have such a room or rooms (once upon a time, these were the "scullery" and "laundry," haunts of low-ranking domestic servants).

Apart from a few larger items such as the ironing board and vacuum cleaner, most of the many things stored in a utility room are small. It is important therefore to have a clear system of storage that groups like with like in well-labeled containers, be they plastic boxes, drawers, or cupboard shelves. There is also a safety consideration. The utility room is generally where potentially dangerous chemicals such as methylated spirits, bleach, and other cleaning materials are stored. Even if you don't have small children of your own, children may visit, so it is as well to keep these safe. Place them either in a locked cupboard or in one with childproof safety catches screwed to the doors, or in a large safety box of the type that has a secure lid (this applies anywhere in the home, whether or not you have a separate utility room).

There are also messy things such as shoe-cleaning equipment in a utility room. These too need to be kept well out of the way of little fingers. Buckets and mops can clutter a utility room and are best stored at or near floor level, as they tend to be wet. Other wet things stored in a utility room include such items as dishcloths and tea towels waiting to be washed. Separate these from dry washing and store until wash day in a bucket with a lid, such as a diaper pail bought from a baby supplies shop, perhaps in a pre-wash solution or eco-friendly bleach substitute.

Clean, dry laundry waiting to be ironed needs an easily accessible storage space in the utility room, and one that is capable of accommodating a pile that grows as the week progresses towards ironing day. Dry and hang shirts on coat hangers, rather than folding them into this pile, and you will find they have fewer creases to iron out when the time comes. Store them on hooks on the back of the door and on the wall, alongside your collection of wire coat hangers awaiting another laundry day.

*An office (left, below, and below bottom)
constructed from modular units. The
desk and shelves are all attached to metal
"ladders," which support them. You can
have just one column, with two supports,
or several, as here. This desk closes up to
conceal the contents of pigeonholes, but
the stacking trays remain in view.*

THE HOME OFFICE

ALMOST EVERY MODERN HOME has some form of home office. Home offices come in two types. The first is in a room that serves another function as well, such as a dining room or spare bedroom. It may be a place for occasional professional work, or it may be dedicated entirely to household affairs. It can be no more than a desk tucked away in a corner or fitted into a recess, where you pay bills and keep records.

The minimum you need (in addition to the desk) includes a filing cabinet for storing such items as travel and medical documents, bills, and papers relating to your personal finances. You also need storage for stationery, telephone books, address books, and records noting who gave and received what presents for Christmas and birthdays. A computer provides you with the opportunity to have much of this information in paperless form. It will take up less room but will not always be as instantly accessible as in a file on a shelf.

Because so many people now have home offices, and indeed the appearance of many offices outside the home is lively and contemporary, modern office furniture is wonderfully varied. No longer are filing cabinets a compulsory gray or brown metal — some are spray-painted pink, blue or green, others are built in wooden casings, others are made of shiny stainless steel. Likewise, a desk can be found or made to contribute to any style of interior, as can storage boxes. A handy way of storing office and computer equipment and stationery is in boxes on a cart (also any style) that can be wheeled out from under one end of the desk when needed.

An alternative is to have the entire office hidden in cupboards and drawers that are part of the room's overall storage system. In a dining room, surround the office area with bookcases and enclose the clutter with doors faced with faux book spines or wallpaper printed with books. In a spare room, the office can be concealed in a wardrobe – open a door and there is your desk.

A smart working corner with plain white shelves carrying rows of identical black magazine and file boxes (above). The desk and chair are black too, and the clock is black and white. Leaving the wall around the clock bare lightens the effect.

Paint brushes (below) should ideally be stored hung from the holes in their handles. This does not necessarily require an elaborate arrangement. Opposite page: Computer disks stored handily in a pouch.

In either case, it is vital to have an adjustable, supportive office chair that will help prevent back pain and repetitive stress injuries, rather than one which simply suits the room's decorative scheme. The position of a computer is also important. The keyboard should be just above your lap height and the screen angled so that it does not create reflective glare. An adjustable computer table or stand is ideal.

At the other end of the scale is the second type of home office, a separate room in which to conduct paid work as well as household affairs. This might be an entire section of your home given over to creative business, where you and your employees or colleagues earn a living. More usual is a single room with desk, filing drawers, shelves for storing books and other reference material, computer, telephone, answering machine and so on. This type of room used to be called a "study," suggesting pseudo-scholarly activities taking place in leisure time. Today, it is undoubtedly an office, a businesslike place more likely to have a fax machine and modem than leather-bound volumes and cigars.

Whatever your size and type of office, try to keep your desk tidy and, ideally, clear it when you finish work each time. A row of cubbyholes across the wall directly above your desk will help you do this. Do not use them all for storage; keep some free for work in progress, which you can retrieve when you next sit down to work. Clearing your desk each day could be described as a form of "hot desking." A management technique designed to help keep your mind clear and prevent you getting bogged down in routine and detail, "hot desking" as used in offices means that no one has his or her own desk – you sit wherever there is a space when you arrive at work that day.

THE WORKBENCH

THE CELLAR, workshop, or garage is a likely site for a workbench, where tools and supplies for crafts, decorating, home maintenance, and hobbies like cabinetmaking and furniture restoration are stored. If you are lucky, you have a well-lit outbuilding or studio for these activities.

Keep tools clean and orderly. The most popular method for doing this is to have a board fixed to the wall or sticking up from the back of the workbench, supplied with appropriate hooks, clips, and brackets for your items of equipment. This is a form of up storage: getting things up off the workbench. Draw a clear outline for each tool when it is up on the board, remove the item, and paint over the line with a color that contrasts with the board so that you can see at a glance where each tool belongs. Screws, nails, hinges, and other small objects are best kept in transparent containers for quick and accurate identification.

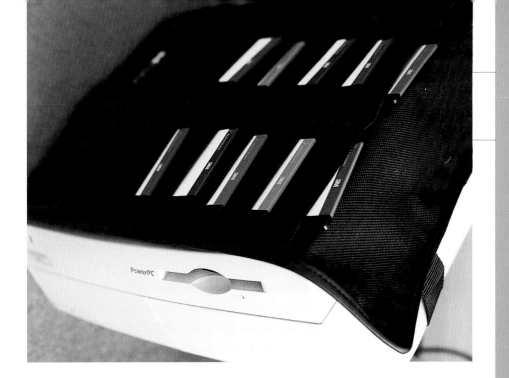

CREATIVE SPACE

Creative activities and crafts may be a hobby or a business – either way you need a work space in which to pursue them and sufficient storage for materials and equipment.

Plan for expansion when you calculate how much storage space you need to keep everything in order, and consider the scale of the items to be stored when planning how to divide the available space.

Sewing things, for example, need many shallow trays or drawers for spools of thread, buttons, and so on, in addition to larger spaces for a sewing machine, cutting table, and other equipment.

Small units of clear-plastic drawers of the type intended for nails, screws, and small tools in a workshop are useful because they are transparent. You also need somewhere to keep patterns and projects in progress.

Remember too to include a bookshelf – every creative activity benefits from the supply of information and inspiration that books, magazines, and other literature provide – and shelves for stacking your collection of fabrics.

Art activities need storage space not only for materials and equipment but also for the many cleaning materials that are involved. These can be toxic and should be stored with appropriate care for safety. Finished artwork that is drying or curing can take up a large amount of space, so allow for this when calculating your storage needs. Special racks of the type often used in schools are available for storing work on paper while it is drying.

IDEA BOX

TIPS FOR EFFICIENT WORKROOMS

* Set up a system of clearly labeled boxes for all the little things sorted in a utility room: bulbs, batteries, polishes, etc.

* Keep cleaning materials, chemicals, and messy items secure.

* Have a plastic bin or other container for storing dirty things waiting for wash day.

* Have space for a growing supply of clean, dry folded laundry awaiting ironing day.

* Dry and store shirts waiting to be ironed on hangers so they have fewer creases.

* The home office, whether for household management, earning a living, or both, needs a filing system for storing papers.

* It also needs storage space for some or all of the following: stationery, directories and reference material, computer/fax/modem.

* If your home office is a desk in a corner, use a cart for storage, keeping it under the desk when you are not working there.

* If your office shares the dining room or spare room, conceal it in cupboards or bookshelves or behind a screen.

* Keep your desk clear of clutter – cubbyholes on the wall above will help.

* Color-code old cardboard boxes by painting the outsides different shades of the same color for a sophisticated effect to create an inexpensive filing system.

* Keeping things orderly and accessible will help you have a clear mind at work.

INDEX

ACKNOWLEDGMENTS

Key

RM   Ray Main
LH   Laura Hodgson
CH   Christine
      Hanscomb
EWA   Elizabeth Whiting
      Associates
IA   The Interiors
      Archive
A   Abode

1: Conran Shop
2: RM
3: RM
5: LH
6: IA (*Schulenberg*)
8: A (*Trevor Richards*)
9: LH
10: *top* EWA (*Jean-Paul Bonhommet*), *bottom* CH
11: A (*Ian Parry*)
12: LH
13: LH
14: EWA (*Tim Street Porter*)
15: *top* A (*Paul Barker*); *bottom* EWA (*Friedhalm Thomas*)
16: *top* LH; *bottom* EWA (*Julian Nieman*)
17: A (*Ian Parry*)
22: RM
23: RM
24: *left and right* RM
25: RM
26: LH
27: RM
28: LH
29: LH
30: RM
31: RM
32: *top left* LH; *bottom left and right* RM
33: RM
34: RM
35: *top left, top right, bottom left* RM; *bottom left* LH
36: LH
37: LH
38: LH
39: LH
40: LH
41: IA (*Henry Wilson*)
42: *left and bottom right* LH; *top right* RM
43: *top* EWA; *bottom left and right* LH
44: LH
45: LH
46: *left* EWA (*Rodney Hyett*); *right* LH
47: LH
48: LH

49: LH
50: LH
51: LH
52: RM
53: LH
54: IA (*Schulenberg*)
55: RM
56: IA (*Simon Brown*)
57: LH
58: RM
59: A (*Ian Parry*)
60: RM
61: RM
62: RM
63: RM
64: LH
65: IA (*Andrew Wood*)
66: LH
67: A (*Tim Morris*)
68: *left* EWA (*Elizabeth Whiting*); *right* EWA (*Neil Lorimer*)
70: RM
71: RM
72: RM
73: RM
74: *top* LH; *bottom* EWA (*Spike Powell*)
75: A (*Ian Parry*)
76: EWA (*Jean-Paul Bonhommet*)
77: *top left and top right* LH; *bottom* Thomas Dobbie (*Azumi*)
78: IA (*Cecilia Innes*)
79: LH
80: RM
81: RM
82: RM
83: RM
84: RM
85: RM
86: RM
87: RM
88: RM
89: RM
90: Martin Moore and Co.
91: RM
92: *top* IA (*James Mortimer*); *bottom* IA (*James Mortimer*)
93: IA (*Tim Beddow*)
94: LH
95: LH
96: RM
97: RM
98: RM
99: RM
100: RM
101: RM
102: *left* RM; *right* Martin Moore and Co.
103: Martin Moore and Co.
104: *top* EWA (*Rodney

Hyett*); *bottom* IA (*Jacques Dirand*)
105: A (*Ian Parry*)
106: LH
107: LH
108: EWA (*Jon Bouchier*)
109: LH
110: LH
111: IA (*Tim Beddow*)
112: RM
113: RM
114: IA (*Simon Brown*)
115: IA (*Simon Brown*)
116: LH
117: LH
118: *left* LH; *right* A (*Ian Parry*)
119: EWA (*Spike Powell*)
120: RM
121: *top* A (*Ian Parry*); *bottom* IA (*Simon Brown*)
122: A (*Trevor Richards*)
123: LH
124: LH
125: LH
126: RM
127: RM
128: RM
129: RM
130: *top* CH; *bottom* LH
131: CH
132: RM
133: RM
134: LH
135: LH
136: IA (*J.Pilkington*)
137: LH
138: RM
139: A (*Ian Parry*)
140: RM
141: RM
142: *top left* RM; *bottom left* CH; *right* RM
143: LH
144: LH
145: EWA (*Jean-Paul Bonhommet*)
146: IA (*J. Pilkington*)
147: *left and right*: IA (*Brian Harrison*)
148: *left* IA (*Tim Beddow*); *right* EWA (*Jean-Paul Bonhommet*)
149: A (*Chris Grayson*)
150: RM
151: LH
152: LH
153: LH
154: LH
155: LH
156: *top* IA (*Henry Wilson*); *bottom* EWA (*Jean-Paul Bonhommet*)
157: LH

The publishers would like to thank the following people:

Isabel Brunner

Emma & Niccolo Caderni

Henry Chancellor

The late David Hicks

Philip Jones

Thomas & Karin Jones

Alya Khalidi

Anbara Khalidi

Katrina Lithgow

Joyce Mason

Paula and Mark West

and the following companies:

Jason Cooper Architects
14 Alexander Street
London W2 5NT
0171 727 3104
see pages: 130 (bottom) 143

Designer's Guild
267–271 Kings Road
London SW3 5EN
0171 243 7300

Alannah Dowling
9 Gertrude Street
London SW10 0NJ
see pages: 77 110

David Mellor
4 Sloane Square
London SW1W 8EE
0171 730 4259

The Holding Company
244–245 Kings Road
London SW3 5EL
0171 352 1600

Littman Goddard Hogarth Architects
12 Chelsea Wharf
15 Lots Road
London SW10 0QJ
0171 315 7871
see pages: 25 30 33 42 (top right) 58 60 (left) 70–73 128 129

Douglas Mackie
10 The Paramount Building
212 St John Street
London EC1V 4PH
0171 253 5266
see pages: 135 137

Martin Moore and Company
36 Church Street
Altrincham
Cheshire WA14 4DW
0161 928 2643
see pages: 90 102 (top right) 103

Ocean
Mail order: 0800 132 985

Purves & Purves
81–83 Tottenham Court Road
London W1P 9HD
0171 580 8223

Shaker
322 Kings Road
London SW3 5UH
0171 352 3918
see pages: 22 23 85 100 120

Dean Smith of
MCH Architects
11 Chelsea Wharf
15 Lots Road
London SW10 0QJ
0171 376 5754
see pages: 135 137 152 153